Table of Contents

P9-DYE-053

From Back, Left to Right:
Alyson Haynes, Margaret Dickey,
Tamara Goldis, Callie Nash,
Leah Van Deren, Stefanie Maloney,
Catherine Steele, Karen Rankin,
Wendy Ball, Victoria Cox,
Elizabeth Austin

AMERICA'S **BEST** RECIPES

simple
Weeknight
150 delicious everyday recipes
meals

OXMOOR HOUSE®

Chicken with Ratatouille, page 28

WELCOME

In the *America's Best* Test Kitchen, we recognize how your fast-paced life has redefined the way you cook and shaped your choice of recipes. That's why we've streamlined ingredient lists and methods, as well as broadened our use of convenience products to bring you recipes that are easy to prepare and still taste delicious. Our Test Kitchen tastes thousands upon thousands of recipes each year allowing only the best of the best to pass onto the pages of our cookbooks. We showcase the easiest to make, best-loved, and most satisfying recipes selected by our kitchen and approved by home cooks.

We've made it even easier by arranging our chapters to fit your busy schedule—and even highlighted our top 5 favorite recipes in each and every chapter. Start by following our Top Ten Test Kitchen Tips that will help you get dinner on the table even faster. If you're short on time, try our 30-Minute Recipes or Slow-Cooker Surprises. Or, pick up a deli roasted chicken at the grocery store and prepare one of our Sensational Sidekicks. And, you can't go wrong with Pizza & Pasta Dishes.

In addition to chapters that fit the way you cook, we've included great tips from our Test Kitchen staff's years of experience throughout the pages. Not only that, but we also have tips from the community of cooks who have prepared our tasty recipes in their own kitchens. And, discover how to make a recipe even easier with our shortcut secrets.

Our Test Kitchen has done all the work so that you can connect with friends and family around the dinner table.

Enjoy your cooking!

Elizabeth Austin

Elizabeth Austin
America's Best Recipes
Test Kitchen Director

1

Quick & Easy Meal Planning

Follow these essential tips to make weeknight cooking and menu planning even easier.

TOP 10 TIPS
for an Organized Kitchen

1 Store wooden spoons, rubber and metal spatulas, tongs, wire whisks, cooking spoons, and kitchen shears in a jar near your cooktop and mixing center. Store pot holders close to the oven, cooktop, and microwave for quick access.

2 Keep knives sharpened and stored in a safe, convenient holder on the countertop or in a drawer.

3 Save counter space by using stackable canisters for flour, sugar, and coffee. Keep a set of measuring cups and spoons in the flour and sugar containers.

4 Keep a salad spinner on hand to spin lettuce and other vegetables until dry.

5 Organize your recipe files. Try those recipes you've been saving, and discard those you know you'll never use. Make a separate file for quick-and-easy recipes.

6 Place bottles and boxes in your cupboard on a pullout tray where you can easily see the ingredients that you need.

7 Keep a swivel-bladed vegetable peeler handy for tasks other than peeling vegetables. Use it to shred a small amount of cheese, remove strings from celery stalks, or make quick chocolate curls.

8 Store a cutting board on the counter near the sink, ready for use at a moment's notice.

9 Have 2 sets of both dry and liquid measuring cups and spoons on hand so you can measure consecutive ingredients without repeatedly washing or wiping out the measure.

10 Stock your pantry and refrigerator with staple items. Group similar staples together, rotating older ones to the front to use first. Keep as many labels as possible in view for at-a-glance inventory.

TOP (10) TIPS
for Meal Planning and Grocery Shopping

1 **Good-quality convenience foods save time:** For example, make your special potato casserole, but combine it with deli roasted chicken, a frozen ready-to-steam vegetable mix, and pop-and-bake rolls.

2 **Jump-start your next meal:** Grill extra chicken to add to a salad, turn into chicken salad, or use for quesadillas another night. Double a spaghetti sauce recipe, and freeze the surplus in single-serving portions.

3 **Oven management:** If all dishes are cooked in the oven at different temperatures, rethink the menu plan.

4 **Dining in shifts:** If family members eat at different times, you need foods that hold well. If using the microwave, reheat using 60% to 70% power. It takes longer, but the heating will be more even, and the food will taste fresher.

5 **The dish on casseroles:** Stock casseroles in your freezer without tying up your dishes. Line each dish with heavy-duty aluminum foil. Cover and freeze finished casserole 2 to 3 hours. Lift the frozen casserole from the dish and freeze in a zip-top plastic freezer bag.

6 **Cleanup:** To avoid hand-cleaning pans, line baking sheets with parchment paper, and cook veggies in microwave-safe serving dishes.

7 **Buy just what you need:** Scan recipes to determine what on-hand ingredients you already have and any special cooking equipment you'll need.

8 **Organize your grocery list by category:** meat, dairy, produce, canned goods, frozen foods, breads, and so on. Make a template for your grocery list on your computer. Establish a set of abbreviations for commonly purchased items to use as shorthand on your list: pt (paper towels), chix (chicken), mjc (Monterey Jack cheese), etc.

9 **Shop in order:** select nonperishables first (usually the aisles), then move to the perimeter of the store to pick up the perishables.

10 **Organize your shopping cart:** At the checkout stand, group nonrefrigerated items together and refrigerated items together. This way, like items will be bagged together for easy unpacking at home.

2

30-Minute Recipes

*Put down the take-out menu,
and bring new meaning to
the term fast food with these
easy-to-prepare dishes.*

1 lb. skinned and boned chicken breasts, cut into thin strips
$^1/_2$ tsp. table salt
$^1/_4$ cup cornstarch
4 Tbsp. vegetable oil, divided
$^1/_2$ lb. Broccolini, cut into 1-inch pieces
1 cup chicken broth, divided
1 red bell pepper, cut into thin strips
1 small yellow squash, thinly sliced into half moons
$^1/_4$ cup sliced green onions
2 tsp. cornstarch
1 Tbsp. fresh lime juice
$1^1/_2$ tsp. soy sauce
1 tsp. Asian chili-garlic sauce
Hot cooked rice

TOP **5** 30-MINUTE RECIPES

Chicken-and-Veggie Stir-fry

MAKES: 4 servings
HANDS-ON TIME: 30 min.
TOTAL TIME: 30 min.

1 Sprinkle chicken with salt; toss with $^1/_4$ cup cornstarch.

2 Stir-fry chicken in 3 Tbsp. hot oil in a large skillet or wok over medium-high heat 5 to 6 minutes or until golden brown and done. Transfer to a plate, using a slotted spoon; keep warm. Add Broccolini and $^1/_4$ cup broth; cover and cook 1 to 2 minutes or until crisp-tender. Transfer to plate with chicken, using slotted spoon.

3 Add remaining 1 Tbsp. oil to skillet. Sauté bell pepper and next 2 ingredients in hot oil 2 minutes or until crisp-tender.

4 Whisk together 2 tsp. cornstarch and remaining $^3/_4$ cup broth until cornstarch dissolves. Add broth mixture, chicken, and Broccolini (with any accumulated juices) to bell pepper mixture in skillet. Cook, stirring often, 1 minute or until liquid thickens. Stir in lime juice and next 2 ingredients. Serve over hot cooked rice.

community chat

If you have zucchini and mushrooms on hand then you can add them to the recipe for a colorful presentation.

TOP 5 30-MINUTE RECIPES

Green Bean Pasta Salad with Lemon-Thyme Vinaigrette

MAKES: 4 to 6 servings
HANDS-ON TIME: 15 min.
TOTAL TIME: 30 min.

test kitchen note

Casarecce [cah-sah-RECH-ee] pasta looks similar to a scroll with the long sides curled inward toward the center.

12 oz. uncooked casarecce pasta*
1/2 lb. haricots verts (thin green beans), cut in half lengthwise
1 Tbsp. fresh thyme
5 tsp. lemon zest, divided
1/4 cup finely chopped roasted, salted pistachios
2 Tbsp. Champagne vinegar
1 Tbsp. minced shallots
1 garlic clove, minced
1 tsp. table salt
1/2 tsp. freshly ground black pepper
5 Tbsp. olive oil
1 1/2 cups loosely packed arugula
Topping: Freshly shaved Parmesan cheese

❶ Cook pasta according to package directions, adding green beans to boiling water during last 2 minutes of cooking time; drain. Rinse pasta mixture with cold running water; drain well.

❷ Place pasta mixture, thyme, and 3 tsp. lemon zest in a large bowl; toss gently to combine.

❸ Whisk together pistachios, next 5 ingredients, and remaining 2 tsp. lemon zest in a small bowl. Add oil in a slow, steady stream, whisking constantly until blended. Drizzle over pasta mixture. Add arugula, and toss gently to coat. Top with Parmesan, if desired.

* Penne pasta may be substituted.

NOTE: We tested with Whole Foods Market Organic Casarecce pasta.

TOP **5** 30-MINUTE RECIPES

Black Bean Chili

MAKES: 4 servings
HANDS-ON TIME: 30 min.
TOTAL TIME: 30 min.

make it a meal

Serve this with a grilled pimiento cheese sandwich. Lightly spread 2 slices of bread with mayonnaise. Spread deli pimiento cheese on 1 side of a white bread slice; top with another bread slice. Repeat with remaining pimiento cheese and mayonnaise for desired number of sandwiches. Cook, in batches, on a hot griddle or large nonstick skillet over medium heat, gently pressing with a spatula, 4 to 5 minutes on each side or until golden brown and cheese is melted.

3 (15-oz.) cans black beans, divided
1 large sweet onion, chopped
1 (12-oz.) package meatless burger crumbles
2 Tbsp. vegetable oil
4 tsp. chili powder
1 tsp. ground cumin
$1/2$ tsp. black pepper
$1/4$ tsp. table salt
2 (14.5-oz.) cans petite diced tomatoes with jalapeños
1 (14-oz.) can low-sodium fat-free chicken broth
Garnish: sliced jalapeño peppers

1 Drain and rinse 2 cans black beans. (Do not drain third can.)

2 Sauté chopped onion and burger crumbles in hot oil in a large Dutch oven over medium heat 6 minutes. Stir in chili powder and next 3 ingredients; sauté 1 minute. Stir in diced tomatoes, chicken broth, and drained and undrained beans. Bring to a boil over medium-high heat; cover, reduce heat to low, and simmer, stirring occasionally, 10 minutes.

NOTE: We tested with Boca Meatless Ground Crumbles. For extra flavorful toppings, try sour cream, shredded Cheddar cheese, lime wedges, chopped fresh cilantro, chopped tomatoes, and corn chips.

Grab the skewers, fire up the grill, and enjoy these easy and delicious kabobs, great for any night of the week.

20	fresh thick asparagus spears
40	sea scallops (about $1^{1}/_{2}$ lb.)
10	(6-inch) wooden skewers
$^{1}/_{4}$	cup herb-flavored olive oil
	Lemon wedges

1 Preheat grill to 350° to 400° (medium-high) heat. Snap off and discard tough ends of asparagus. Cut asparagus into 2-inch pieces. Thread scallops alternately with asparagus pieces onto each skewer. Brush with olive oil.

2 Grill kabobs, covered with grill lid, $2^{1}/_{2}$ minutes on each side or just until scallops are opaque. Sprinkle with salt to taste. Serve kabobs with lemon wedges.

NOTE: We tested with Benissimo Mediterranean Garlic Gourmet oil.

TOP **5** 30-MINUTE RECIPES

Grilled Scallop Kabobs

MAKES: 4 to 6 servings

HANDS-ON TIME: 30 min.

TOTAL TIME: 30 min.

make it a meal

Round out the meal with grilled pita wedges and deli tabbouleh salad.

1 (20-oz.) package refrigerated four-cheese ravioli*

1 (16-oz.) jar sun-dried tomato Alfredo sauce

2 Tbsp. white wine

2 medium tomatoes, chopped**

1/2 cup chopped fresh basil

1/3 cup grated Parmesan cheese

Garnish: fresh basil strips

❶ Prepare pasta according to package directions.

❷ Meanwhile, pour Alfredo sauce into a medium saucepan. Pour wine into sauce jar; cover tightly, and shake well. Stir wine mixture into saucepan. Stir in chopped tomatoes and 1/2 cup chopped basil, and cook over medium-low heat 5 minutes or until thoroughly heated. Toss with pasta, and top evenly with grated Parmesan cheese.

* 1 (13-oz.) package three-cheese tortellini may be substituted.
** 1 (14.5-oz.) can petite diced tomatoes, fully drained, may be substituted.

NOTE: We tested with Buitoni Four Cheese Ravioli and Classico Sun-dried Tomato Alfredo Pasta Sauce.

TOP **5** 30-MINUTE RECIPES

Tuscan Pasta with Tomato-Basil Cream

MAKES: 4 to 6 servings

HANDS-ON TIME: 15 min.

TOTAL TIME: 15 min.

community chat

This recipe is so good and fast! You can use mushroom ravioli instead of cheese and regular Alfredo sauce instead of the sundried tomato one. This is a great way to dress up Alfredo sauce.

Santa Fe Skillet Casserole

MAKES: 6 servings
HANDS-ON TIME: 10 min.
TOTAL TIME: 15 min.

test kitchen note

Substituting Mexican-seasoned burger-style crumbles for plain crumbles adds an extra kick to this one-dish meal.

1 (12-oz.) package meatless burger crumbles
1 cup chopped onion (about 1)
1 cup chopped green bell pepper (about 1)
2 Tbsp. vegetable oil
1 1/2 cups uncooked instant rice (such as Uncle Ben's 5-Minute Rice)
1 1/2 cups vegetable broth
1/4 tsp. table salt
1/4 tsp. black pepper
1 (14.5-oz.) can Mexican-style stewed tomatoes, undrained
3/4 cup (3 oz.) shredded (2%) reduced-fat sharp Cheddar cheese

❶ Sauté first three ingredients in hot oil in a large Dutch oven over medium heat 6 minutes.

❷ Stir in rice and next 4 ingredients. Cover, reduce heat, and simmer 5 minutes or until rice is tender and liquid is absorbed. Sprinkle with cheese; serve immediately.

3 whole wheat bread slices

2 Tbsp. self-rising yellow cornmeal mix

1/2 tsp. ground cumin

8 thinly sliced boneless pork loin chops (about 1 1/4 lb.)

1/2 tsp. table salt

1/4 tsp. black pepper

1 large egg

2 Tbsp. whole grain mustard

1/4 cup olive oil

Cumin-Crusted Pork Cutlets

MAKES: 4 to 6 servings

HANDS-ON TIME: 27 min.

TOTAL TIME: 27 min.

1 Preheat oven to 200°. Process bread in a food processor until finely crumbled. Combine breadcrumbs, cornmeal mix, and cumin in a shallow bowl.

2 Sprinkle pork chops with salt and pepper. Whisk together egg, mustard, and 2 Tbsp. water until blended. Dip pork in egg mixture; dredge in breadcrumb mixture, pressing to adhere.

3 Cook half of pork in 2 Tbsp. hot oil in a large nonstick skillet over medium heat 3 to 4 minutes on each side or until golden brown. Keep warm in a 200° oven. Repeat procedure with remaining pork and oil. Serve warm.

shortcut secret

Make several batches of fresh breadcrumbs ahead and freeze them for use in this recipe and others.

Pork Fried Rice

MAKES: 6 servings
HANDS-ON TIME: 30 min.
TOTAL TIME: 30 min.

shortcut secret

You can make the ready rice ahead of time. In fact, chilling the rice will help keep it from clumping while stir-frying. Use leftover rice, or prepare 1 (8-oz.) pouch ready-to-serve jasmine rice according to package directions, and chill.

1 lb. boneless pork chops, cut into strips
$^1/_2$ tsp. black pepper
1 Tbsp. sesame oil, divided
$^3/_4$ cup diced carrots
$^1/_2$ cup chopped onion
3 green onions, chopped
1 Tbsp. butter
2 large eggs, lightly beaten
2 cups cooked long-grain white or jasmine rice, chilled
$^1/_2$ cup frozen English peas, thawed (optional)
$^1/_4$ cup soy sauce
Garnishes: green onion, carrot

❶ Season pork with pepper. Cook pork in $1^1/_2$ tsp. hot oil in a large skillet over medium heat 7 to 8 minutes or until done. Remove pork from skillet.

❷ Heat remaining $1^1/_2$ tsp oil in skillet; sauté carrots and onion in hot oil 2 to 3 minutes or until tender. Stir in green onions, and sauté 1 minute. Remove mixture from skillet. Wipe skillet clean.

❸ Melt butter in skillet. Add eggs to skillet, and cook, without stirring, 1 minute or until eggs begin to set on bottom. Gently draw cooked edges away from sides of pan to form large pieces. Cook, stirring occasionally, 30 seconds to 1 minute or until thickened and moist. (Do not overstir.) Add pork, carrot mixture, rice, and, if desired, peas to skillet; cook over medium heat, stirring often, 2 to 3 minutes or until thoroughly heated. Stir in soy sauce. Serve immediately.

Our nod to the Virginia wine country and Thomas Jefferson's love of pasta.

- 2 (8.8-oz.) packages strozzapreti pasta
- 1/4 lb. country ham, cut into 1/8-inch-thick strips (about 3/4 cup)
- 2 Tbsp. olive oil
- 3 shallots, thinly sliced
- 8 oz. assorted wild mushrooms, sliced
- 1 garlic clove, thinly sliced
- 1 cup Viognier or dry white wine
- 1/2 cup frozen sweet peas
- 1/3 cup coarsely chopped fresh flat-leaf parsley
- 1/4 cup heavy cream
- 3 Tbsp. butter
- 1/4 tsp. black pepper
- 1 cup freshly grated pecorino Romano cheese

"Jefferson" Virginia Ham Pasta

MAKES: 6 to 8 servings

HANDS-ON TIME: 30 min.

TOTAL TIME: 30 min.

❶ Prepare pasta according to package directions.

❷ Meanwhile, sauté ham in hot oil in a large skillet over medium heat 2 minutes or until lightly browned and crisp. Add shallots; sauté 1 minute. Add mushrooms and garlic, and cook, stirring often, 2 minutes or until mushrooms are tender. Stir in wine, and cook 5 minutes or until reduced by half.

❸ Add peas, next 4 ingredients, and 1/2 cup cheese, stirring until cheese begins to melt and cream begins to thicken. Stir in hot cooked pasta, and toss until coated. Serve immediately with remaining 1/2 cup cheese.

NOTE: We tested with Jefferson Vineyards Viognier.

community chat

If you can't find the strozzapreti pasta, use penne rigate.

Skillet Sausage 'n' Rice

MAKES: 4 to 6 servings
HANDS-ON TIME: 10 min.
TOTAL TIME: 30 min.

- 1 (16-oz.) package smoked sausage
- 1 medium-size green bell pepper, chopped
- 1 small onion, chopped
- 1 garlic clove, minced
- 1 cup chicken broth
- 2 (3.5-oz.) bags quick-cooking brown rice
- $1/2$ tsp. table salt
- $1/4$ tsp. black pepper
  Garnish: chopped fresh parsley

❶ Cut sausage into $1/2$-inch-thick slices. Sauté in a large nonstick skillet over medium-high heat 8 to 10 minutes or until lightly browned. Remove sausage slices, and drain on paper towels, reserving 1 Tbsp. drippings in skillet.

❷ Add bell pepper, onion, and garlic to skillet, and sauté over medium-high heat 4 minutes or until tender. Add chicken broth, stirring to loosen browned bits from bottom of skillet, and bring to a boil. Remove rice from cooking bags; add rice, sausage, salt, and black pepper to skillet. Reduce heat to medium-low, cover, and cook 5 minutes or until rice is tender.

test kitchen note

Shop for green bell peppers that have bright colors and taut skins. Make sure that the peppers are firm and sturdy, avoiding peppers that show signs of decay. Peppers can be found all year long, but are most abundant during the summer months.

Chicken with Ratatouille

MAKES: 6 servings
HANDS-ON TIME: 30 min.
TOTAL TIME: 30 min.

test kitchen note

Feel free to substitute whatever is overflowing in your garden or at the market for the vegetables in the ratatouille.

1 small red onion, chopped
$^1/_2$ (1-lb.) eggplant, peeled and chopped
2 Tbsp. olive oil
2 small summer squash, chopped
2 garlic cloves, minced
1 medium-size red bell pepper, chopped
1 medium tomato, diced
$^1/_4$ cup chopped fresh basil
$1^1/_4$ tsp. kosher salt, divided
$^3/_4$ tsp. freshly ground pepper, divided
6 (4-oz.) chicken breast cutlets
$^1/_3$ cup all-purpose flour
1 cup canola oil
Garnish: fresh basil leaves

❶ Sauté onion and eggplant in hot olive oil in a large nonstick skillet over medium-high heat 5 minutes or until tender and light brown around edges. Add squash, garlic, and bell pepper; sauté 5 minutes or until tender. Add tomato, basil, and $^1/_4$ tsp. each kosher salt and freshly ground black pepper. Cook, stirring constantly, 2 to 3 minutes or until mixture is thoroughly heated.

❷ Remove vegetable mixture from skillet. Cover loosely with aluminum foil to keep warm. Wipe skillet clean. Rinse chicken, and pat dry. Sprinkle with 1 tsp. salt and $^1/_2$ tsp. black pepper. Dredge chicken in flour, shaking off excess.

❸ Fry chicken, in 2 batches, in hot canola oil in skillet over medium-high heat 2 to 3 minutes on each side or until golden brown and done. Drain on a wire rack over paper towels; cover and keep warm. Transfer to a serving dish, and top with vegetable mixture.

1 cup mayonnaise
1/4 cup chopped fresh cilantro
6 Tbsp. white wine vinegar, divided
3/4 tsp. table salt, divided
1/8 tsp. black pepper
4 skinned and boned chicken breasts (about 1 lb.)

4 ears fresh corn, husks removed
1/4 cup melted butter
1 (10-oz.) package shredded coleslaw mix
3 Tbsp. olive oil
1/2 tsp. sugar
1/4 tsp. black pepper

Grilled Chicken with Corn and Slaw

MAKES: 4 servings
HANDS-ON TIME: 30 min.
TOTAL TIME: 30 min.

❶ Combine mayonnaise, cilantro, 3 Tbsp. vinegar, 1/4 tsp. salt, and 1/8 tsp. pepper in a small bowl. Reserve 3/4 cup mayonnaise mixture. Brush chicken with remaining 1/4 cup mayonnaise mixture.

❷ Preheat grill to 350° to 400° (medium-high) heat. Grill chicken and corn at the same time, covered with grill lid. Grill chicken 7 to 10 minutes on each side or until done; grill corn 14 to 20 minutes or until done, turning every 4 to 5 minutes and basting with melted butter.

❸ Toss coleslaw mix with oil, sugar, and remaining 3 Tbsp. vinegar, 1/2 tsp. salt and 1/4 tsp pepper. Season chicken and corn with salt and pepper to taste. Serve with coleslaw and reserved mayonnaise mixture.

make it a meal

Dice leftover grilled chicken, and then combine with leftover slaw for a tasty lunch.

1 (1-lb.) turkey tenderloin, cut into thin strips
2 tsp. sesame oil, divided
1 cup chicken broth
4 garlic cloves, minced
$1\frac{1}{2}$ Tbsp. cornstarch
$\frac{1}{4}$ tsp. dried crushed red pepper
$\frac{1}{4}$ tsp. table salt
1 red bell pepper, cut into thin strips
2 cups fresh broccoli florets
1 (8-oz.) can sliced water chestnuts, drained
2 Tbsp. soy sauce
2 cups hot cooked rice

Garlic Turkey-Broccoli Stir-Fry

MAKES: 4 servings
HANDS-ON TIME: 6 min.
TOTAL TIME: 14 min.

❶ Stir-fry turkey in 1 tsp. hot oil in a large skillet or wok over medium-high heat 5 minutes or until lightly browned. Remove turkey from skillet, and set aside.

❷ Combine broth and next 4 ingredients in a small bowl, stirring until smooth. Set aside.

❸ Add remaining 1 tsp. oil to skillet. Add pepper strips and broccoli; stir-fry 1 minute.

❹ Add water chestnuts; stir-fry 30 seconds. Increase heat to high. Return turkey to skillet. Stir in broth mixture, soy sauce, and any accumulated juices. Bring to a boil; cook 1 to 2 minutes or until slightly thickened. Serve over rice.

shortcut secret

If you can't find turkey tenderloin for the stir-fry, use turkey cutlets or Butterball's fresh turkey breast, which is already cut into strips.

Greek Turkey Cutlets and Pasta

MAKES: 4 servings
HANDS-ON TIME: 26 min.
TOTAL TIME: 26 min.

test kitchen note

Feel free to substitute your favorite canned tomato blend.

$\frac{1}{2}$ (16-oz.) package fettuccine
1 lb. turkey cutlets
1 tsp. Greek seasoning, divided
$\frac{1}{4}$ cup all-purpose flour
5 Tbsp. olive oil, divided
$\frac{1}{2}$ cup chopped red onion
1 (14$\frac{1}{2}$-oz.) can diced tomatoes with balsamic vinegar, basil, and olive oil, undrained
1 (3.8-oz.) can sliced black olives, drained
$\frac{1}{2}$ cup crumbled feta cheese
Garnish: chopped fresh parsley

❶ Prepare pasta according to package directions. Meanwhile, sprinkle cutlets with $\frac{3}{4}$ tsp. Greek seasoning. Dredge in flour.

❷ Cook half of cutlets in 1$\frac{1}{2}$ Tbsp. hot oil in a large non-stick skillet over medium-high heat 3 minutes on each side or until done. Repeat procedure with remaining cutlets and 1$\frac{1}{2}$ Tbsp. oil. Remove cutlets from skillet, and drain on paper towels, reserving drippings in skillet.

❸ Heat remaining 2 Tbsp. oil in skillet with drippings over medium heat; add onion and remaining $\frac{1}{4}$ tsp. Greek seasoning, and sauté 2 to 3 minutes or until tender. Stir in tomatoes and olives; cook 1 minute or until tender. Remove from heat, and toss in hot cooked pasta until blended.

❹ Transfer pasta mixture to a serving bowl; sprinkle with half of cheese. Top with cutlets and remaining cheese. Garnish, if desired.

This Indian-style meal comes together very quickly and feels like a nice treat.

Curried Rice with Shrimp

MAKES: 4 servings

HANDS-ON TIME: 25 min.

TOTAL TIME: 25 min.

- 2 Tbsp. olive oil
- 1 large onion, finely chopped
- 2 carrots, thinly sliced
- 2 russet potatoes, peeled and cut into 1-inch cubes
- 2 garlic cloves, minced
- 2 tsp. curry powder
- 1 cup uncooked long-grain white rice
- 2$\frac{1}{2}$ cups chicken broth
- $\frac{1}{2}$ tsp. black pepper
- 1 lb. medium-size raw shrimp, peeled and deveined
- $\frac{1}{4}$ cup chopped fresh basil or 2 tsp. dried

❶ Heat oil in a large skillet over medium heat. Add onion, carrot, and potato to hot oil; cook, stirring occasionally, 6 to 8 minutes. or until vegetables start to soften.

❷ Add garlic and curry powder; cook, stirring until fragrant, about 2 minutes. Add rice, broth, and black pepper. Bring to a boil. Cover; reduce heat to medium-low, and simmer 15 minutes.

❸ Stir in shrimp. Cover and cook, stirring occasionally, about 5 to 7 minutes until shrimp turn pink and rice is tender. Sprinkle with basil, and serve immediately.

test kitchen note

Add more curry powder if you like things spicy.

1 lb. peeled, large raw shrimp

1 (12-oz.) package angel hair pasta

1/2 cup butter

1/4 cup finely chopped onion

3 garlic cloves, finely chopped

1 tsp. salt-free herb-and-spice seasoning

1 tsp. Worcestershire sauce

1 Tbsp. fresh lemon juice

1/4 cup freshly grated Romano or Parmesan cheese

1 Tbsp. chopped fresh parsley

Shrimp Scampi

MAKES: 4 servings

HANDS-ON TIME: 20 min.

TOTAL TIME: 30 min.

❶ Devein shrimp, if desired.

❷ Prepare pasta according to package directions.

❸ Meanwhile, melt butter in a large nonstick skillet over medium-high heat; add onion and garlic, and sauté 3 to 5 minutes or until tender. Stir in seasoning and sauce.

❹ Reduce heat to medium. Add shrimp, and cook, stirring occasionally, 3 to 5 minutes or just until shrimp turn pink. Stir in lemon juice. Toss shrimp mixture with pasta, and sprinkle with cheese and parsley. Serve immediately.

NOTE: We tested with Mrs. Dash Italian Medley Seasoning Blend.

community chat

This is absolutely wonderful! It was so easy, especially when you devein the shrimp, chop the onion and garlic, grate the cheese, and mince the parsley early in the day. Serve this with a small green salad and garlic bread.

Spicy Catfish with Vegetables and Basil Cream

MAKES: 4 servings
HANDS-ON TIME: 30 min.
TOTAL TIME: 30 min.

3 Tbsp. butter, divided
1 (16-oz.) package frozen whole kernel corn, thawed
1 medium onion, chopped
1 medium-size green bell pepper, chopped
1 medium-size red bell pepper, chopped
3/4 tsp. table salt
3/4 tsp. black pepper
4 (6-oz.) catfish fillets
1/2 cup plus 2 Tbsp. all-purpose flour, divided
1/4 cup plain yellow cornmeal
1 Tbsp. Creole seasoning
1/3 cup buttermilk
1 Tbsp. vegetable oil
1/2 cup whipping cream
2 Tbsp. chopped fresh basil

❶ Melt 2 Tbsp. butter in a large skillet over medium-high heat. Add corn, onion, and bell peppers; sauté 6 to 8 minutes or until tender. Stir in salt and black pepper; spoon onto a serving dish, and keep warm.

❷ Dredge fillets in 2 Tbsp. flour. Combine 1/2 cup flour, cornmeal, and Creole seasoning in a large shallow bowl. Dip fillets in buttermilk, and dredge in flour mixture; shake off excess.

❸ Cook fillets, in 2 batches, in 1/2 Tbsp. butter and oil (per batch) 2 to 3 minutes on each side or until fillets flake with a fork. Remove fillets from skillet, and arrange over vegetables.

❹ Add cream to skillet, stirring to loosen browned bits from bottom of skillet. Add chopped basil, and cook, stirring often, 1 to 2 minutes or until thickened. Serve basil cream with fillets and vegetables.

shortcut secret

The key when breading fish is to use one hand for the wet ingredients and one hand for the dry. Dip a fillet in the milk (or wet mixture); then with your dry hand, dredge the fillet in the flour. This technique prevents your hands from becoming covered in breading mixture.

Easy Skillet Pimiento Mac 'n' Cheese

MAKES: 6 servings
HANDS-ON TIME: 10 min.
TOTAL TIME: 20 min.

$^1/_2$ (16-oz.) package penne pasta
2 Tbsp. all-purpose flour
$1^1/_2$ cups 1% low-fat milk
1 cup (4 oz.) shredded sharp Cheddar cheese
1 (4-oz.) jar diced pimiento, drained
$^3/_4$ tsp. table salt
$^1/_4$ tsp. black pepper
Pinch of paprika

❶ Prepare pasta according to package directions.

❷ Whisk together flour and $^1/_4$ cup milk. Add flour mixture to remaining milk, whisking until smooth.

❸ Bring milk mixture to a boil in a large skillet over medium heat; reduce heat to medium-low, and simmer, whisking constantly, 3 to 5 minutes or until smooth. Stir in cheese and next 4 ingredients until smooth. Stir in pasta, and cook 1 minute or until thoroughly heated. Serve immediately.

Easy Skillet Green Chile Mac 'n' Cheese:

Substitute 1 cup (4 oz.) shredded Monterey Jack cheese for Cheddar cheese and 1 (4-oz.) can chopped green chiles, undrained, for diced pimiento. Proceed with recipe as directed.

Easy Skillet Whole Grain Mac 'n' Cheese:

Substitute $^1/_2$ (13.5-oz.) package whole grain penne pasta for regular. Proceed with recipe as directed.

community chat

This is a super-easy upgrade of a classic using penne pasta instead of elbow macaroni. And, it has a quick cooking time as a skillet meal.

This quick dish gets a smoky flavor boost from packaged pre-grilled tofu.

Thai Fried Rice with Tofu

MAKES: 4 servings

HANDS-ON TIME: 26 min.

TOTAL TIME: 26 min.

2 tsp. peanut oil

2 tsp. jarred minced ginger

1 tsp. jarred minced garlic

$^1/_2$ tsp. dried crushed red pepper

1 (9.2-oz.) package grilled tofu, cut into $^1/_2$-inch cubes

$^1/_4$ cup sweetened flaked coconut, toasted

1 Tbsp. light brown sugar

1 large egg, lightly beaten

3 cups coarsely chopped bok choy (about 1 large head)

$1^1/_2$ cups frozen cut green beans, thawed

$^1/_4$ cup chopped dry-roasted salted cashews

2 cups chilled cooked jasmine or basmati rice

2 Tbsp. soy sauce

❶ Heat oil in a large nonstick skillet over medium-high heat. Add ginger and next 3 ingredients; sauté 3 minutes, stirring occasionally. Add coconut and brown sugar; cook 1 minute. Push tofu mixture to one side of pan. Add egg to empty side of pan; stir-fry 1 to 2 minutes or until soft-scrambled.

❷ Add bok choy, green beans, and cashews, and cook 5 minutes or until vegetables are tender, stirring occasionally. Stir in rice and soy sauce, and cook 2 minutes or until thoroughly heated.

shortcut secret

If you have any kind of leftover cooked rice from another meal, you may substitute it for the jasmine rice, if desired.

1 (16-oz.) package linguine

1 (7-oz.) jar sun-dried tomatoes in oil

3 garlic cloves, minced

1/4 cup extra virgin olive oil

1 (4-oz.) package crumbled feta cheese

2 Tbsp. thin fresh basil strips

1/4 cup pine nuts, toasted

Linguine with Sun-Dried Tomatoes

MAKES: 6 servings
HANDS-ON TIME: 26 min.
TOTAL TIME: 26 min.

❶ Prepare linguine according to package directions.

❷ Drain tomatoes, reserving 2 Tbsp. oil. Cut tomatoes into thin strips.

❸ Sauté garlic in 2 Tbsp. reserved oil and olive oil in skillet over medium heat 1 minute or until garlic is fragrant. Stir in tomatoes, and remove from heat.

❹ Toss together tomato mixture, hot cooked pasta, feta cheese, and basil in a large bowl. Sprinkle with toasted pine nuts.

Linguine with Tuna and Sun-Dried Tomatoes:

Prepare recipe as directed. Stir in 2 (6-oz.) aluminum foil pouches solid white tuna chunks, drained, and 1 (3-oz.) can sliced black olives, drained.

shortcut secret

Cut sun-dried tomatoes in a hurry by using kitchen shears.

Change the level of spiciness by adjusting the amount of dried crushed red pepper.

Cheese Ravioli with Spicy Tomato Sauce

1 cup ricotta cheese
$^1/_2$ cup freshly shredded Parmesan cheese
$^3/_4$ tsp. black pepper
$^1/_3$ cup chopped fresh basil, divided
$^1/_2$ (16-oz.) package wonton wrappers
1 pt. cherry tomatoes, halved

2 Tbsp. olive oil
$^1/_2$ cup chicken broth
1 tsp. white wine vinegar
$^1/_4$ to $^1/_2$ tsp. dried crushed red pepper
$^1/_4$ tsp. table salt
Garnishes: fresh basil leaves, freshly shaved Parmesan cheese

MAKES: 4 servings
HANDS-ON TIME: 30 min.
TOTAL TIME: 30 min.

❶ Stir together first 3 ingredients and 3 Tbsp. chopped fresh basil in a small bowl.

❷ Arrange 1 wonton wrapper on a clean, flat surface. (Cover remaining wrappers with plastic wrap or a damp towel to prevent drying out.) Lightly moisten edges of wrapper with water. Place about $1^1/_2$ tsp. cheese mixture in center of wrapper; fold 2 opposite corners together over cheese mixture, forming a triangle. Press edges together to seal, removing any air pockets. Cover with plastic wrap or a damp cloth. Repeat procedure with remaining wrappers and cheese mixture.

❸ Cook ravioli, in 2 batches, in boiling salted water to cover in a Dutch oven over medium-high heat 3 minutes. Remove with a slotted spoon, and drain well on a lightly greased wire rack. Divide cooked ravioli among 4 individual serving bowls.

❹ Sauté tomatoes in hot oil in a large skillet over medium-high heat 2 minutes or just until soft. Add broth and white wine vinegar; cook 2 to 3 minutes or until tomatoes begin to wilt. Stir in red pepper, salt, and remaining basil. Pour sauce over ravioli. Serve immediately.

community chat

The white wine vinegar makes the dish taste superb. You'll definitely want to make it again!

3

Make-Ahead Meals

Make weeknight meals a little easier with dishes you can prepare partially or completely ahead.

- 1 tsp. table salt
- 1 cup plain yellow cornmeal
- 1/2 tsp. Montreal steak seasoning
- 1 cup (4 oz.) shredded sharp Cheddar cheese, divided
- 1 lb. ground chuck
- 1 medium zucchini, cut in half lengthwise and sliced (about 2 cups)
- 1 cup chopped onion
- 1 Tbsp. olive oil
- 2 (14^1/$_2$-oz.) cans petite diced tomatoes, drained
- 1 (6-oz.) can tomato paste
- 2 Tbsp. chopped fresh flat-leaf parsley

Tomato 'n' Beef Casserole with Polenta Crust

MAKES: 6 servings

HANDS-ON TIME: 20 min.

TOTAL TIME: 1 hour, 25 min.

1 Preheat oven to 350°. Bring 3 cups water and salt to a boil in a 2-qt. saucepan over medium-high heat. Whisk in cornmeal; reduce heat to low, and simmer, whisking constantly, 3 minutes or until thickened. Remove from heat, and stir in steak seasoning and 1/4 cup Cheddar cheese. Spread cornmeal mixture into a lightly greased 11- x 7-inch baking dish.

2 Brown ground chuck in a large nonstick skillet over medium-high heat, stirring often, 10 minutes or until meat crumbles and is no longer pink; drain and transfer to a bowl.

3 Sauté zucchini and onion in hot oil in skillet over medium heat 5 minutes or until crisp-tender. Stir in beef, tomatoes, and tomato paste; simmer, stirring often, 10 minutes. Pour beef mixture over cornmeal crust. Sprinkle with remaining 3/4 cup cheese.

4 Bake at 350° for 30 minutes or until bubbly. Sprinkle casserole with parsley just before serving.

Italian Casserole with Polenta Crust:

Substitute Italian sausage for ground chuck and Italian six-cheese blend for Cheddar cheese. Prepare recipe as directed, sautéing 1 medium-size green bell pepper, chopped, with onion in Step 3.

community chat

This recipe is a keeper. This comfort food favorite boasts ingredients that are normally kept on-hand.

TOP **5** MAKE-AHEAD MEALS

Hamburger Steak
with Sweet Onion-Mushroom Gravy

MAKES: 4 servings
HANDS-ON TIME: 35 min.
TOTAL TIME: 35 min.

test kitchen note

To make ahead: Proceed with Step 1 as directed. Wrap each patty individually in plastic wrap, and place in a large zip-top plastic freezer bag. Freeze up to 3 months. Thaw frozen patties in refrigerator 8 hours; proceed with Steps 2 and 3.

2 honey-wheat bread slices
1 lb. ground round
1 large egg, lightly beaten
2 garlic cloves, minced
1/2 tsp. table salt
1/2 tsp. freshly ground pepper
1 (1.2-oz.) envelope brown gravy mix
1 Tbsp. vegetable oil
1 (8-oz.) package sliced fresh mushrooms
1 medium-size sweet onion, halved and thinly sliced

❶ Process bread slices in a food processor 10 seconds or until finely chopped. Place breadcrumbs in a mixing bowl; add ground round and next 4 ingredients. Gently combine until blended, using your hands. Shape into 4 (4-inch) patties.

❷ Whisk together brown gravy mix and 1 1/2 cups water.

❸ Cook patties in hot oil in a large nonstick skillet over medium-high heat 2 minutes on each side or just until browned. Remove patties from skillet. Add mushrooms and onion to skillet, and sauté 6 minutes or until tender. Stir in prepared gravy, and bring to a light boil. Return patties to skillet, and spoon gravy over each patty. Cover, reduce heat to low, and simmer 8 to 10 minutes.

3 cups chopped cooked chicken

2 cups (8 oz.) shredded pepper Jack cheese*

1/2 cup sour cream

1 (4.5-oz.) can chopped green chiles, drained

1/3 cup chopped fresh cilantro

8 (8-inch) soft taco-size flour tortillas

Vegetable cooking spray

1 (8-oz.) bottle green taco sauce

1 (8-oz.) container sour cream

Toppings: chopped tomatoes, chopped avocado, sliced green onions, sliced black olives, coarsely chopped fresh cilantro

Chicken Enchiladas

MAKES: 4 to 6 servings

HANDS-ON TIME: 15 min.

TOTAL TIME: 45 min.

❶ Preheat oven to 350°. Stir together first 5 ingredients in a large bowl. Spoon about 1/2 cup chicken mixture down center of each tortilla; roll up tortillas.

❷ Place rolled tortillas, seam sides down, in a lightly greased 13- x 9-inch baking dish. Lightly coat tops of tortillas with cooking spray.

❸ Bake at 350° for 30 to 35 minutes or until golden brown.

❹ Stir together taco sauce and sour cream. Spoon over hot enchiladas, and sprinkle with desired toppings.

* Monterey Jack cheese may be substituted.

shortcut secret

Prepare recipe as directed through Step 2. Cover with aluminum foil, and chill overnight, or freeze up to 1 month. If frozen, thaw in refrigerator overnight. Let stand at room temperature 30 minutes. Proceed with recipe as directed in Steps 3 and 4.

12 oz. pizza dough
3 cups Zesty Pizza Sauce
1/4 cup turkey pepperoni slices
1 1/2 cups (6 oz.) shredded part-skim mozzarella cheese

1 Preheat oven to 450°. Stretch pizza dough into 3 (12-inch) circles. Place on lightly greased baking sheets.

2 Spread one-third Zesty Pizza Sauce on each pizza crust, leaving a 1-inch border. Top each with pepperoni slices. Sprinkle with cheese.

3 Bake pizza at 450° for 20 minutes or until crust is golden and cheese is melted.

Zesty Pizza Sauce

MAKES: 3 cups
HANDS-ON TIME: 20 min.
TOTAL TIME: 1 hour, 35 min.

1 large onion, chopped
4 garlic cloves, minced
1 Tbsp. olive oil
1 (28-oz.) can diced tomatoes
1 Tbsp. dried Italian seasoning
3/4 tsp. table salt
1/2 tsp. black pepper
1/4 tsp. dried crushed red pepper

1 Sauté onion and garlic in hot olive oil in a 3-qt. sauce-pan over medium-high heat 10 minutes or until tender. Stir tomatoes, Italian seasoning, salt, pepper, and crushed red pepper into onion mixture. Bring to a boil; reduce heat to low, and simmer, stirring occasionally, 1 hour. Let stand 15 minutes. Process tomato mixture in a blender or food processor, in batches, until smooth. Cover and chill up to 5 days. Reheat in a saucepan over medium-low heat.

TOP **5** MAKE-AHEAD MEALS

Pepperoni Pizza

MAKES: 6 servings
HANDS-ON TIME: 5 min.
TOTAL TIME: 25 min.

test kitchen note

To Freeze It: Cover pizzas tightly with plastic wrap, and wrap with aluminum foil; label and freeze up to 1 month. To prepare, remove from freezer, and thaw in fridge overnight. Bake as directed in Step 3.

2 cups fresh black-eyed peas
8 cherry tomatoes, halved
1/2 cup diced assorted bell peppers
1/4 small red onion, thinly sliced (about 1/4 cup)
3 Tbsp. rice vinegar
1 Tbsp. Creole mustard
3/4 cup canola oil, divided
1/2 tsp. freshly ground black pepper, divided
1/2 tsp. kosher salt, divided
4 (6-oz.) skin-on redfish, grouper, or snapper fillets
1 tsp. chopped fresh thyme
2 Tbsp. thinly sliced fresh basil, divided
2 cups loosely packed baby arugula
8 pickled okra, halved
2 lemons, halved

Sautéed Redfish

MAKES: 4 servings
HANDS-ON TIME: 50 min.
TOTAL TIME: 2 hours, 50 min.

❶ Cook peas, covered, in boiling salted water to cover 20 minutes or until tender. Remove peas from heat, and let stand, covered, 10 minutes. Drain and rinse with cold water. Combine cooked peas, tomatoes, bell peppers, and onion in a large bowl.

❷ Whisk together vinegar, mustard, 1/2 cup oil, 1/4 tsp. black pepper, and 1/4 tsp. salt. Stir 1/2 cup vinaigrette into pea mixture, reserving remaining vinaigrette. Cover and chill pea mixture 1 1/2 to 24 hours.

❸ Rub both sides of fillets with 1 Tbsp. oil; sprinkle with remaining 1/4 tsp. each black pepper and salt. Press thyme and 1 Tbsp. basil leaves onto flesh side of fish.

❹ Heat remaining 3 Tbsp. oil in a large nonstick skillet over medium heat. Place fish, flesh sides down, in hot oil; cook 3 minutes or until golden. (Do not allow herbs to burn.) Turn fish; cook 4 minutes or just until fish flakes with a fork.

❺ Stir arugula and remaining 1 Tbsp. basil into pea salad; divide salad among 4 plates. Top each with a fish fillet. Serve with pickled okra, lemon halves, and remaining 1/4 cup vinaigrette.

make it a meal

Serve this flavorful sautéed fish over a black-eyed pea salad that you can make ahead.

1 lb. ground sirloin*
1 lb. ground pork
   sausage
1 sleeve multigrain
   saltine crackers,
   crushed
1 (15-oz.) can tomato
   sauce
1 green bell pepper,
   diced
1/2 cup diced red onion
2 large eggs, lightly
   beaten
   Chunky Red Sauce

Beef-and-Sausage Meatloaf
with Chunky Red Sauce

MAKES: 12 servings (2 meatloaves)

HANDS-ON TIME: 15 min.

TOTAL TIME: 1 hour, 15 min., not including sauce

❶ Preheat oven to 425°. Line bottom and sides of 2 (8- x 4-inch) loaf pans with aluminum foil, allowing 2 to 3 inches to extend over sides. Lightly grease foil.

❷ Gently combine first 7 ingredients in a medium bowl. Shape mixture into 2 loaves. Place meatloaves in prepared pans.

❸ Bake at 425° for 50 minutes or until a meat thermometer inserted into thickest portion registers 160°. Let stand 10 minutes. Remove meatloaves from pans, using foil sides as handles. Serve with Chunky Red Sauce.

* Ground chuck or lean ground beef may be substituted.

NOTE: If serving 1 meatloaf, let remaining cooked meatloaf stand until completely cool (about 30 minutes). Wrap tightly in plastic wrap and aluminum foil, and place in a large zip-top plastic bag. Refrigerate in an air-tight container up to 2 to 3 days, or freeze up to 1 month.

shortcut secret

Serve one meatloaf for supper, and freeze the other for a meal later in the month.

Chunky Red Sauce:

Stir together 1 jar vegetable spaghetti sauce, 1 can fire-roasted diced tomatoes*, 1 tsp. dried Italian seasoning, and ¼ tsp. black pepper in a large saucepan over medium heat. Cook, stirring frequently, 15 minutes or until thoroughly heated. **MAKES:** about 3 cups; **HANDS-ON TIME:** 20 min.; **TOTAL TIME:** 20 min.

* 1 (14.5-oz.) can diced tomatoes may be substituted.

NOTE: We tested with Ragu Garden Combination Pasta Sauce and Hunt's Fire Roasted Diced Tomatoes.

Italian Meatballs

MAKES: 30 meatballs (6 to 8 servings)

HANDS-ON TIME: 20 min.

TOTAL TIME: 55 min.

- 1/2 lb. mild Italian sausage, casings removed
- 3/4 lb. ground turkey
- 1 cup fine, dry breadcrumbs
- 3/4 cup minced onion
- 4 large eggs, lightly beaten
- 3/4 cup grated Parmesan cheese
- 1 Tbsp. minced garlic
- 2 tsp. dried Italian seasoning
- 1/2 tsp. table salt
- 1/2 tsp. black pepper
- 6 cups Marinara Sauce
- Hot cooked spaghetti
- Freshly grated Parmesan cheese (optional)

❶ Combine first 10 ingredients in a large bowl until well blended.

❷ Gently shape meat mixture into 30 (1 1/2-inch) balls.

❸ Bring Marinara Sauce to a boil in a Dutch oven over medium heat, stirring occasionally; reduce heat to low, and simmer. Add 10 meatballs, and cook 6 to 8 minutes over low heat or until meatballs are done. Remove meatballs from sauce, and keep warm; repeat procedure with remaining meatballs.

❹ Return all cooked meatballs to sauce, reduce heat to low, and cook 10 more minutes.

❺ Serve over hot cooked spaghetti, and, if desired, sprinkle with Parmesan cheese.

Marinara Sauce

MAKES: about 6 cups

HANDS-ON TIME: 15 min.

TOTAL TIME: 15 min.

- 1 cup beef broth
- 1/2 cup dry red wine
- 1 (26-oz.) jar marinara sauce
- 1 (8-oz.) can tomato sauce with basil, garlic, and oregano

❶ Stir together beef broth, wine, 1/2 cup water, marinara sauce, and tomato sauce. Cook over medium heat, stirring occasionally, 10 minutes or until thoroughly heated.

shortcut secret

Make a large batch of these, and freeze them in meal-size portions to cook during the week.

Creamy Ham Casserole

MAKES: 8 servings
HANDS-ON TIME: 8 min.
TOTAL TIME: 38 min.

8 oz. uncooked egg noodles
1 (10³/₄-oz.) can cream of mushroom soup
1 (8-oz.) container chive-and-onion-flavored cream cheese, softened
²/₃ cup milk
2 cups chopped baked glazed ham
1¹/₂ cups fresh broccoli florets
1 (9-oz.) package frozen asparagus, thawed
6 baby carrots, chopped
2 cups (8 oz.) shredded mozzarella cheese
1 cup (4 oz.) shredded Cheddar cheese
¹/₂ cup crushed seasoned croutons

❶ Preheat oven to 400°. Cook pasta according to package directions.

❷ Stir together soup, cream cheese, and milk in a large bowl. Stir in pasta, ham, and next 3 ingredients. Spoon half of ham mixture into 2 lightly greased 8-inch square baking dishes.

❸ Combine cheeses. Sprinkle half of cheese mixture over casseroles. Spoon remaining ham mixture over cheeses.

❹ Combine remaining cheese mixture with croutons. Sprinkle over casseroles.

❺ Bake casserole at 400° for 30 minutes or until lightly browned.

test kitchen note

This recipe can be made ahead and frozen. Wrap casserole in heavy-duty aluminum foil; label and freeze up to 1 month. Thaw frozen casserole in the fridge overnight. Bake, uncovered, at 400° for 35 to 40 minutes.

Pizza Spaghetti Casserole

MAKES: 6 servings

HANDS-ON TIME: 30 min.

TOTAL TIME: 1 hour, 10 min.

- 12 oz. uncooked spaghetti
- $\frac{1}{2}$ tsp. table salt
- 1 (1-lb.) package mild ground pork sausage
- 2 oz. turkey pepperoni slices (about 30), cut in half
- 1 (26-oz.) jar tomato-and-basil pasta sauce
- $\frac{1}{4}$ cup grated Parmesan cheese
- 2 cups (8-oz.) shredded Italian three-cheese blend

❶ Preheat oven to 350°. Cook spaghetti with salt according to package directions. Drain well, and place in a lightly greased 13- x 9-inch baking dish.

❷ Brown sausage in a large skillet over medium-high heat, stirring occasionally, 5 minutes or until meat crumbles and is no longer pink. Drain and set aside. Wipe skillet clean. Add pepperoni, and cook over medium-high heat, stirring occasionally, 4 minutes or until slightly crisp.

❸ Top spaghetti in baking dish with sausage; pour pasta sauce over sausage. Arrange half of pepperoni slices over pasta sauce. Sprinkle with cheeses. Arrange remaining half of pepperoni slices over cheese.

❹ Cover casserole with nonstick or lightly greased aluminum foil. Bake at 350° for 30 minutes; remove foil, and bake 10 more minutes or until cheese is melted and just begins to brown.

shortcut secret

Use kitchen shears to quickly slice the pepperoni in half.

Chicken Enchilada Dip

MAKES: 8 servings

HANDS-ON TIME: 10 min.

TOTAL TIME: 4 hours, 10 min.

2 (10-oz.) cans mild green chile enchilada sauce, divided

10 (6-inch) fajita-size corn tortillas, torn into 3-inch pieces

4 cups pulled cooked chicken breasts

1½ cups sour cream

1 (12 oz.) package shredded colby-Jack cheese blend

1 (10¾-oz.) can cream of mushroom soup

8 cups shredded iceberg lettuce

1 (15-oz.) can black beans, drained and rinsed

3 tomatoes, diced

❶ Spoon ½ cup enchilada sauce over bottom of a greased 4-qt. slow cooker. Add enough tortilla pieces to cover sauce.

❷ Stir together chicken, sour cream, 2 cups cheese, and soup. Spread 2 cups chicken mixture over tortilla pieces. Top with tortilla pieces to cover. Drizzle with ½ cup enchilada sauce. Repeat layers twice, ending with tortilla pieces and remaining enchilada sauce. Sprinkle with remaining 1 cup cheese.

❸ Cover and cook on LOW 4 hours. Place lettuce on plates; top with chicken, beans, and tomatoes. Serve hot.

test kitchen note

The corn tortillas cook into this dish and thicken it. You won't see them after they're cooked, but you will still taste their authentic Mexican flavor.

Slow-cooked Barbecued Chicken

MAKES: 6 servings

HANDS-ON TIME: 20 min.

TOTAL TIME: 5 hours, 20 min.

- 2 tsp. table salt
- 1½ tsp. paprika
- ½ tsp. garlic powder
- ½ tsp. black pepper
- 1 (3- to 3½-lb.) cut-up whole chicken
- ½ cup cola soft drink
- ⅓ cup ketchup
- ¼ cup firmly packed light brown sugar
- 2 Tbsp. apple cider vinegar
- 2 Tbsp. bourbon
- 1 lemon, sliced

❶ Stir together first 4 ingredients in a small bowl. Sprinkle over chicken. Place chicken in a single layer in a lightly greased 6-qt. slow cooker.

❷ Whisk together cola soft drink and next 4 ingredients in a small bowl. Slowly pour mixture between chicken pieces (to avoid removing spices from chicken). Place lemon slices in a single layer on top of chicken.

❸ Cover and cook on HIGH 5 hours (or on LOW 6½ to 7½ hours) or until done.

❹ Transfer chicken pieces to a serving platter; discard lemon slices. Skim fat from pan juices in slow cooker. Pour pan juices over chicken; serve immediately.

NOTE: To make ahead, cool shredded chicken completely. Freeze in an airtight container up to 3 months. Serve on cornbread topped with coleslaw, if desired.

community chat

You can omit the bourbon, and this recipe will still be delicious. The meat just falls off the bones. And, it's so easy to make.

Classic Chicken Tetrazzini

MAKES: 8 servings

HANDS-ON TIME: 20 min.

TOTAL TIME: 55 min.

- $1^1/_2$ (8-oz.) packages vermicelli
- $^1/_2$ cup butter
- $^1/_2$ cup all-purpose flour
- 4 cups milk
- $^1/_2$ cup dry white wine
- 2 Tbsp. chicken bouillon granules
- 1 tsp. seasoned pepper
- 2 cups (8 oz.) freshly grated Parmesan cheese, divided
- 4 cups diced cooked chicken
- 1 (6-oz.) jar sliced mushrooms, drained
- $^3/_4$ cup slivered almonds

1 Preheat oven to 350°. Prepare pasta according to package directions.

2 Meanwhile, melt butter in a Dutch oven over low heat; whisk in flour until smooth. Cook 1 minute, whisking constantly. Gradually whisk in milk and wine; cook over medium heat, whisking constantly, 8 to 10 minutes or until mixture is thickened and bubbly. Whisk in bouillon granules, seasoned pepper, and 1 cup Parmesan cheese.

3 Remove from heat; stir in chicken, mushrooms, and hot cooked pasta.

4 Spoon mixture into a lightly greased 13- x 9-inch baking dish; sprinkle with slivered almonds and remaining 1 cup Parmesan cheese.

5 Bake at 350° for 35 minutes or until bubbly.

community chat

This dish is absolutely decadent. The sauce is so rich, and the almonds on top add a delightful flavor.

Slow-Cooker Turkey Chili

MAKES: 4 to 6 servings
HANDS-ON TIME: 20 min.
TOTAL TIME: 6 hours, 20 min.

make it, a meal

Serve this with cornbread or tortilla chips.

1$\frac{1}{4}$ lb. lean ground turkey
1 large onion, chopped
1 garlic clove, minced
1 (1.25-oz.) envelope chili seasoning mix
1 (12-oz.) can beer
1$\frac{1}{2}$ cups frozen whole kernel corn, thawed
1 red bell pepper, chopped
1 green bell pepper, chopped
1 (28-oz.) can crushed tomatoes
1 (15-oz.) can black beans, drained and rinsed
1 (8-oz.) can tomato sauce
$\frac{3}{4}$ tsp. table salt
Toppings: shredded Cheddar cheese, finely chopped red onion, sliced fresh jalapeño peppers

❶ Cook first 4 ingredients in a large skillet over medium-high heat, stirring often, 8 minutes or until turkey crumbles and is no longer pink. Stir in beer, and cook 2 minutes, stirring occasionally.

❷ Spoon mixture into a 5$\frac{1}{2}$-qt. slow cooker; stir in corn and next 6 ingredients until well blended. Cover and cook on LOW 6 hours. Serve with desired toppings.

- 2 lb. unpeeled, large raw shrimp
- 1/4 cup butter
- 1 small red onion, chopped*
- 1/2 cup chopped red bell pepper*
- 1/2 cup chopped yellow bell pepper*
- 1/2 cup chopped green bell pepper*
- 4 garlic cloves, minced
- 2 cups fresh or frozen sliced okra
- 1 Tbsp. lemon juice
- 1 1/2 tsp. salt
- 3 cups cooked long-grain rice
- 1 (10 3/4-oz.) can cream of shrimp soup
- 1/2 cup dry white wine
- 1 Tbsp. soy sauce
- 1/2 tsp. ground red pepper
- 1/4 cup grated Parmesan cheese

Cajun Shrimp Casserole

MAKES: 6 servings

HANDS-ON TIME: 30 min.

TOTAL TIME: 1 hour, 6 min.

❶ Preheat oven to 350°. Peel shrimp; devein, if desired.

❷ Melt butter in a large skillet over medium-high heat. Add onion and next 3 ingredients; sauté 7 minutes or until tender. Add garlic; sauté 1 minute. Stir in okra, lemon juice, and salt; sauté 5 minutes. Add shrimp; cook 3 minutes or until shrimp turn pink. Stir in rice and next 4 ingredients until blended. Pour into a lightly greased 11- x 7-inch baking dish. Sprinkle with Parmesan cheese.

❸ Bake at 350° for 15 to 20 minutes or until casserole is bubbly and cheese is lightly browned.

* 1 (10-oz.) package frozen chopped onions and peppers may be substituted.

shortcut secret

To make ahead, cover tightly, label, and freeze unbaked casserole, omitting cheese. To prepare, thaw in the fridge overnight, and let stand at room temperature 30 minutes before baking. Bake, covered, at 350° for 50 minutes. Uncover; sprinkle with Parmesan cheese, and bake 10 more minutes or until cheese is lightly browned.

1 lb. Perfect Poached Shrimp
4 oranges, sectioned
1 large red bell pepper, thinly sliced
1/2 small red onion, sliced
1/2 cup chopped fresh cilantro
1/4 cup chopped fresh mint

Citrus Vinaigrette
2 cups chopped romaine lettuce
2 medium avocados, cubed

Marinated Shrimp Salad with Avocado

MAKES: 6 servings

HANDS-ON TIME: 30 min.

TOTAL TIME: 5 hours, 10 min., including shrimp and vinaigrette

❶ Combine first 6 ingredients in a large bowl; pour Citrus Vinaigrette over shrimp mixture, and gently toss to combine. Cover and chill 4 to 24 hours.

❷ Place lettuce on a platter. Spoon shrimp mixture over lettuce, reserving vinaigrette. Drizzle with reserved vinaigrette. Top with avocado.

Perfect Poached Shrimp

Fill a large bowl halfway with ice and water. Pour 4 qt. water into a Dutch oven; squeeze juice from 1 lemon, halved, into Dutch oven. Stir in lemon halves, 1 Tbsp. black peppercorns, 2 bay leaves, and 2 tsp. salt; bring to a boil over medium-high heat. Remove from heat; add 2 lb. unpeeled, large raw shrimp. Cover and let stand 5 minutes or just until shrimp turn pink. Stir shrimp into ice water; let stand 10 minutes. Peel and devein shrimp. **MAKES:** 3 to 4 servings; **HANDS-ON TIME:** 20 min.; **TOTAL TIME:** 30 min.

Citrus Vinaigrette

Whisk together 1/4 cup fresh orange juice, 1/4 cup olive oil, 1 Tbsp. country-style Dijon mustard, 1 Tbsp. fresh lemon juice, 1/4 tsp. salt, and 1/8 tsp. freshly ground pepper. **MAKES:** about 1/2 cup; **HANDS-ON TIME:** 5 min.; **TOTAL TIME:** 5 min.

shortcut secret

For a quick way to chop herbs, place them in a small glass. Use kitchen shears to cut them into the desired size.

1 (1-lb.) package hot ground pork sausage
2 Tbsp. butter
4 thinly sliced green onions
2 Tbsp. chopped fresh cilantro
14 large eggs, beaten
$^3/_4$ tsp. table salt
$^1/_2$ tsp. black pepper

Cheese Sauce
8 (8-inch) soft taco-sized flour tortillas
1 cup (4 oz.) shredded Monterey Jack cheese with jalapeños
Toppings: halved grape tomatoes, sliced green onions, chopped fresh cilantro

Breakfast Enchiladas

MAKES: 6 to 8 servings

HANDS-ON TIME: 20 min.

TOTAL TIME: 1 hour, 8 min., including cheese sauce

❶ Preheat oven to 350°. Cook sausage in a nonstick skillet over medium-high heat, stirring until sausage crumbles and is no longer pink. Remove from pan; drain well.

❷ Melt butter in a large nonstick skillet over medium heat. Add green onions and cilantro; sauté 1 minute. Add eggs, salt, and pepper; scramble eggs to desired consistency. Remove from heat, and gently fold in $1^1/_2$ cups Cheese Sauce and sausage.

❸ Spoon about $^1/_3$ cup egg mixture down center of each tortilla; roll up. Place, seam side down, in a lightly greased 13- x 9-inch baking dish. Pour remaining Cheese Sauce evenly over tortillas; sprinkle evenly with Monterey Jack cheese. Bake at 350° for 30 minutes or until sauce is bubbly. Serve with desired toppings.

Cheese Sauce

Melt $^1/_3$ cup butter in a heavy saucepan over medium-low heat; whisk in $^1/_3$ cup all-purpose flour until smooth. Cook, whisking constantly, 1 minute. Gradually whisk in 3 cups milk; cook over medium heat, whisking constantly, 5 minutes or until thickened. Remove from heat, and whisk in 2 cups (8 oz.) shredded Cheddar cheese, 1 (4.5-oz.) can chopped green chiles, and $^3/_4$ tsp. salt.
MAKES: about 4 cups; HANDS-ON TIME: 18 min.; TOTAL TIME: 18 min.

test kitchen note

For make-ahead ease, prepare the recipe without baking, and refrigerate overnight. Let stand at room temperature for 30 minutes; bake as directed.

Creamy Egg Strata

MAKES: 8 to 10 servings
HANDS-ON TIME: 35 min.
TOTAL TIME: 10 hours, 10 min.

- 1/2 (16-oz.) French bread loaf, cubed (about 5 cups)
- 6 Tbsp. butter, divided
- 2 cups (8 oz.) shredded Swiss cheese
- 1/2 cup freshly grated Parmesan cheese
- 1/3 cup chopped onion
- 1 tsp. minced garlic
- 3 Tbsp. all-purpose flour
- 1 1/2 cups chicken broth
- 3/4 cup dry white wine
- 1/2 tsp. table salt
- 1/2 tsp. freshly ground black pepper
- 1/4 tsp. ground nutmeg
- 1/2 cup sour cream
- 8 large eggs, lightly beaten

Garnish: chopped fresh chives

❶ Place bread cubes in a well-greased 13- x 9-inch baking dish. Melt 3 Tbsp. butter, and drizzle over bread cubes. Sprinkle with cheeses.

❷ Melt remaining 3 Tbsp. butter in a medium saucepan over medium heat; add onion and garlic. Sauté 2 to 3 minutes or until tender. Whisk in flour until smooth; cook, whisking constantly, 2 to 3 minutes or until lightly browned. Whisk in broth and next 4 ingredients until blended. Bring mixture to a boil; reduce heat to medium-low, and simmer, stirring occasionally, 15 minutes or until thickened. Remove from heat. Stir in sour cream. Add salt and pepper to taste.

❸ Gradually whisk about one-fourth of hot sour cream mixture into eggs; add egg mixture to remaining sour cream mixture, whisking constantly. Pour mixture over cheese in baking dish. Cover with plastic wrap, and chill 8 to 24 hours.

❹ Let strata stand at room temperature 1 hour. Preheat oven to 350°. Remove plastic wrap, and bake 30 minutes or until set. Serve immediately.

community chat

This is an excellent recipe to serve for brunch. It's convenient— as the prep happens a day ahead.

4

Sensational Sidekicks

Round out your dinner with a fabulous salad, your favorite veggies, or the perfect starch.

Lemon-Garlic Green Beans

MAKES: 8 servings
HANDS-ON TIME: 15 min.
TOTAL TIME: 21 min.

A nice switch from green bean casserole or spiced green beans, this dish quickly became a new standard for our family.

$1^{1}/_{2}$ lb. fresh haricots verts (thin green beans), trimmed
2 tsp. table salt, divided
3 garlic cloves, minced
3 shallots, sliced
2 Tbsp. olive oil
$^{1}/_{4}$ cup chopped fresh basil
3 Tbsp. fresh lemon juice
$^{1}/_{4}$ tsp. black pepper
Garnishes: lemon zest, fresh basil leaves

1 Cook beans with 1 tsp. salt in boiling water to cover 4 to 5 minutes or until crisp-tender; drain. Plunge beans into ice water to stop the cooking process; drain.

2 Cook garlic and shallots in hot oil in a large nonstick skillet over medium heat 2 minutes or until just golden brown; remove from heat. Stir in basil, next 2 ingredients, and remaining 1 tsp. salt. Add green beans, and toss to coat. Garnish, if desired.

4 thick bacon slices
3 Tbsp. butter
1 large sweet onion, diced
1 (12-oz.) bottle ale beer
1/2 cup firmly packed brown sugar
1/2 cup bourbon
1 tsp. dried crushed red pepper
6 lb. fresh collard greens, trimmed and chopped
1/2 cup apple cider vinegar
1 tsp. table salt
1/2 tsp. pepper

Bacon-and-Bourbon Collards

MAKES: 10 servings
HANDS-ON TIME: 40 min.
TOTAL TIME: 1 hour, 40 min.

1 Cut bacon crosswise into 1/4-inch strips. Melt butter in a large Dutch oven over medium heat; add bacon, and cook, stirring often, 8 minutes or until crisp. Drain bacon on paper towels, reserving drippings in skillet. Sauté onion in hot drippings 3 minutes or until onion is tender. Stir in bacon, ale, and next 3 ingredients; cook 3 minutes or until mixture is reduced by one-fourth.

2 Add collards, in batches, and cook, stirring occasionally, 5 minutes or until wilted. Reduce heat to medium-low; cover and cook 1 hour or to desired degree of doneness. Stir in vinegar, salt, and black pepper.

test kitchen note

You'll need the largest Dutch oven you have to hold this "mess o' greens." A 7.5-qt. size provides ample space.

Browned butter adds a heavenly toasted nut taste and aroma to traditional mashed potatoes.

- 3/4 cup butter
- 4 lb. Yukon gold potatoes, peeled and cut into 2-inch pieces
- 1 Tbsp. table salt, divided
- 3/4 cup buttermilk
- 1/2 cup milk
- 1/4 tsp. pepper
- Garnishes: chopped fresh parsley, rosemary, thyme

1 Cook butter in a 2-qt. heavy saucepan over medium heat, stirring constantly, 6 to 8 minutes or just until butter begins to turn golden brown. Immediately remove pan from heat, and pour butter into a small bowl. (Butter will continue to darken if left in saucepan.) Remove and reserve 1 to 2 Tbsp. browned butter.

2 Bring potatoes, 2 tsp. salt, and water to cover to a boil in a large Dutch oven over medium-high heat; boil 20 minutes or until tender. Drain. Reduce heat to low. Return potatoes to Dutch oven, and cook, stirring occasionally, 3 to 5 minutes or until potatoes are dry.

3 Mash potatoes with a potato masher to desired consistency. Stir in remaining browned butter, buttermilk, milk, pepper, and remaining 1 tsp. salt, stirring just until blended.

4 Transfer to a serving dish. Drizzle with reserved 1 to 2 Tbsp. browned butter.

NOTE: To make ahead, prepare recipe as directed through Step 3. Place in a lightly greased 2 1/2-qt. ovenproof serving dish; cover and chill up to 2 days. Let stand at room temperature 30 minutes. Preheat oven to 350°, and bake, uncovered, 35 to 40 minutes or until thoroughly heated. Drizzle with reserved browned butter.

TOP 5 SENSATIONAL SIDES

Browned-Butter Mashed Potatoes

MAKES: 6 to 8 servings
HANDS-ON TIME: 35 min.
TOTAL TIME: 55 min.

community chat

The BEST mashed potatoes ever! The secrets to this recipe are the buttermilk and the browned butter. You can mix in a little extra buttermilk to fluff them up a bit.

TOP **5** SENSATIONAL SIDES

Zucchini-Bacon Spoon Bread

MAKES: 8 servings

HANDS-ON TIME: 9 min.

TOTAL TIME: 1 hour, 10 min.

2 cups milk
1 Tbsp. sugar
1 tsp. table salt
$^1/_2$ tsp. freshly ground black pepper
$^1/_8$ tsp. ground red pepper
1 cup plain yellow cornmeal
2 cups shredded zucchini (about 1 large)
1 cup (4 oz.) shredded sharp Cheddar cheese
8 cooked bacon slices, crumbled
2 large eggs, separated
Vegetable cooking spray

1 Preheat oven to 375°. Bring first 5 ingredients to a simmer in a large heavy saucepan over medium-high heat (do not boil); gradually whisk in cornmeal. Cook, stirring constantly, 1 minute or until thick and smooth. Remove from heat, and stir in zucchini, cheese, and bacon. Stir in egg yolks until blended.

2 Beat egg whites at high speed with an electric mixer until stiff peaks form. Stir one-third of egg white mixture into cornmeal mixture. Fold in remaining egg white mixture. Spoon into a $1^1/_2$-qt. soufflé dish or deep baking dish coated with cooking spray.

3 Bake at 375° for 46 to 50 minutes or until top is lightly browned. Serve immediately.

test kitchen note

When making spoon bread, be sure to start with plain cornmeal and not a cornmeal mix, which contains flour, salt, and a leavening agent.

- 1 (16-oz.) package frozen butter beans*
- 4 ears fresh corn, husks removed
- 1 large red onion, cut into thick slices
- 1 large red bell pepper, cut into thick rings
- 3/4 cup mayonnaise
- 3 Tbsp. chopped fresh basil
- 1 garlic clove, pressed
- 1 tsp. table salt
- 1 tsp. Worcestershire sauce
- 1/2 tsp. freshly ground black pepper
- 1 cup halved grape tomatoes

TOP 5 SENSATIONAL SIDES

Grilled Corn-and-Butter Bean Salad

MAKES: 8 to 10 servings

HANDS-ON TIME: 35 min.

TOTAL TIME: 3 hours, 20 min.

❶ Cook butter beans according to package directions; drain and cool completely (about 20 minutes).

❷ Meanwhile, preheat grill to 350° to 400° (medium-high) heat. Grill corn, covered with grill lid, 15 minutes or until done, turning every 4 to 5 minutes. (Some kernels will begin to char and pop.) At the same time, grill onion and bell pepper, covered with grill lid, 5 minutes on each side or until tender. Cool all vegetables completely (about 20 minutes).

❸ Cut kernels from cobs. Discard cobs. Chop onion and bell pepper into 1/2-inch pieces.

❹ Stir together mayonnaise and next 5 ingredients. Stir in butter beans, tomatoes, corn kernels, and onion and pepper pieces. Add salt to taste. Cover and chill 2 to 8 hours before serving. Refrigerate in an airtight container up to 3 days.

* Fresh butter beans may be substituted.

test kitchen note

This grilled corn-and-bean salad is a take on traditional succotash and features butter beans, bell peppers, and tomatoes.

Roasted Orange-Ginger Asparagus

MAKES: 6 to 8 servings
HANDS-ON TIME: 15 min.
TOTAL TIME: 30 min.

make it, a meal

This asparagus dish pairs nicely with a grilled pork tenderloin, cheese grits, and rolls. For a delicious ending, choose one of our desserts beginning on page 254.

2 lb. fresh asparagus
¼ cup orange juice
2 Tbsp. olive oil
1 Tbsp. grated fresh ginger
1 Tbsp. Dijon mustard
½ tsp. table salt
¼ tsp. black pepper
Garnishes: orange zest, orange slice

❶ Preheat oven to 400°. Snap off and discard tough ends of asparagus; place asparagus on a lightly greased baking sheet. Whisk together orange juice, olive oil, and next 4 ingredients; drizzle mixture over asparagus, tossing to coat.

❷ Bake at 400° for 15 minutes or to desired degree of tenderness, turning once after 8 minutes. Garnish, if desired.

1½ cups chicken broth
¼ tsp. table salt
¼ tsp. black pepper
3 Tbsp. butter, divided
1¼ cups uncooked basmati rice
1 small onion, chopped
1 poblano pepper, diced
2 (15-oz.) cans black beans, drained and rinsed
2 tsp. chili powder
1 tsp. ground cumin
1 lime
1 cup toasted sweetened flaked coconut
2 green onions, thinly sliced
½ cup chopped fresh cilantro
Toppings: diced mango, sliced radishes, sliced fresh jalapeño peppers, sour cream

Black Beans and Coconut-Lime Rice

MAKES: 6 servings
HANDS-ON TIME: 35 min.
TOTAL TIME: 48 min.

❶ Bring broth, next 2 ingredients, 2 Tbsp. butter, and 1 cup water to a boil in a 2-qt. saucepan. Stir in rice. Cover, reduce heat to low, and cook 15 to 20 minutes or until rice is tender and water is absorbed.

❷ Meanwhile, melt remaining 1 Tbsp. butter in a medium saucepan over medium-high heat; add onion and poblano pepper, and sauté 5 minutes or until tender. Stir in black beans, chili powder, cumin, and ¾ cup water. Cook over medium-low heat, stirring occasionally, 15 minutes.

❸ Grate zest from lime, avoiding pale bitter pith, into a bowl; squeeze juice from lime into bowl. Fluff rice with a fork. Fold lime zest and juice, coconut, green onions, and cilantro into hot cooked rice. Serve bean mixture over rice with desired toppings.

test kitchen note

To save time, prepare the toasted coconut ahead. Place coconut in a single layer in a shallow pan. Bake at 350° for 5 to 6 minutes or until toasted, stirring occasionally.

1 (4-oz.) package feta cheese, crumbled

1/2 cup chopped dried sweet cherries

1/4 cup chopped fresh flat-leaf parsley

1 tsp. lemon zest

1/2 tsp. dried crushed red pepper

4 Tbsp. olive oil, divided

1 1/2 lb. carrots

1 1/2 lb. parsnips

2 Tbsp. light brown sugar

3 Tbsp. balsamic vinegar

Balsamic-Roasted Carrots and Parsnips

MAKES: 8 to 10 servings

HANDS-ON TIME: 20 min.

TOTAL TIME: 1 hour

1 Preheat oven to 400°. Toss together first 5 ingredients and 1 Tbsp. oil in a small bowl.

2 Cut carrots and parsnips lengthwise into long, thin strips.

3 Whisk together brown sugar, balsamic vinegar, and remaining 3 Tbsp. oil in a large bowl. Toss with carrots and parsnips, and place on a lightly greased 15- x 10-inch jelly-roll pan. Add salt and freshly ground black pepper to taste.

4 Bake at 400° for 40 to 45 minutes or until vegetables are tender and browned, stirring every 15 minutes. Transfer to a serving platter, and gently toss with feta cheese mixture.

community chat

This recipe was easy to make and came together quickly. The colors on the table were beautiful, and the different flavors complemented each other well.

Roasted Carrots with Avocado and Feta Vinaigrette

MAKES: 4 servings
HANDS-ON TIME: 30 min.
TOTAL TIME: 30 min.

- 2 lb. small carrots in assorted colors
- 1 Tbsp. sorghum syrup or honey
- 4 Tbsp. extra virgin olive oil, divided
- 1 tsp. kosher salt
- 1 tsp. ground cumin
- ½ tsp. freshly ground black pepper
- ¼ tsp. dried crushed red pepper
- 1 shallot, minced
- 2 Tbsp. red wine vinegar
- 2 oz. feta, blue, or goat cheese, crumbled
- 1 medium-size ripe avocado, sliced
- 2 Tbsp. fresh cilantro leaves
- 1 Tbsp. roasted, salted, and shelled pepitas (pumpkin seeds)

1 Preheat oven to 500°. Toss carrots with sorghum and 2 Tbsp. oil. Sprinkle with salt and next 3 ingredients; toss to coat. Place carrots in a lightly greased jelly-roll pan. Bake 15 to 20 minutes or until tender, stirring halfway through.

2 Stir together shallot and vinegar. Add salt and pepper to taste. Stir in remaining 2 Tbsp. oil; stir in feta.

3 Arrange carrots and avocado on a serving platter. Drizzle with vinaigrette. Sprinkle with cilantro and pepitas.

test kitchen note

The key to roasting veggies is to use similarly sized pieces. Spread them evenly on a baking sheet, and roast in a very hot oven until just tender.

Cauliflower Gratin with Almond Crust

MAKES: 6 servings

HANDS-ON TIME: 25 min.

TOTAL TIME: 43 min.

shortcut secret

Purchase a container of prechopped onion from the produce section of your grocery store rather than chopping your own.

- 1/4 cup butter
- 1 head cauliflower (about 2 1/4 lb.), separated into florets
- 1 small onion, chopped
- 2 garlic cloves, minced
- 2 Tbsp. all-purpose flour
- 2 tsp. chopped fresh thyme
- 1/2 tsp. table salt
- 1/2 cup whipping cream
- 1 cup (4 oz.) shredded Gruyère cheese
- 2/3 cup Japanese breadcrumbs (panko)
- 1/4 cup sliced almonds
- 1/4 cup grated Parmesan cheese

❶ Preheat oven to 400°. Melt butter in a large skillet over medium-high heat. Add cauliflower and next 2 ingredients; sauté 10 minutes or until golden and just tender. Sprinkle with flour and next 2 ingredients; stir well. Remove from heat.

❷ Spoon cauliflower mixture into an 11- x 7-inch baking dish, and drizzle with cream. Sprinkle with Gruyère cheese and next 3 ingredients.

❸ Bake at 400° for 18 to 20 minutes or until golden.

Peanutty Coleslaw

MAKES: 6 servings

HANDS-ON TIME: 15 min.

TOTAL TIME: 1 hour

- ½ cup chopped fresh cilantro
- ¼ cup chopped green onions
- 3 Tbsp. white vinegar
- 1 Tbsp. sesame oil
- 2 Tbsp. mayonnaise
- 1 tsp. sugar
- 1 tsp. grated fresh ginger
- 2 tsp. wasabi paste
- ½ tsp. table salt
- ½ tsp. black pepper
- 1 (16-oz.) package shredded coleslaw mix
- ¾ cup lightly salted peanuts

1 Whisk together first 10 ingredients in a large bowl; add coleslaw mix, stirring to coat. Cover and chill 1 hour; stir in peanuts just before serving.

test kitchen note

Wasabi paste can be purchased in the Asian section of most supermarkets. If you prefer a creamy coleslaw, double the amount of dressing.

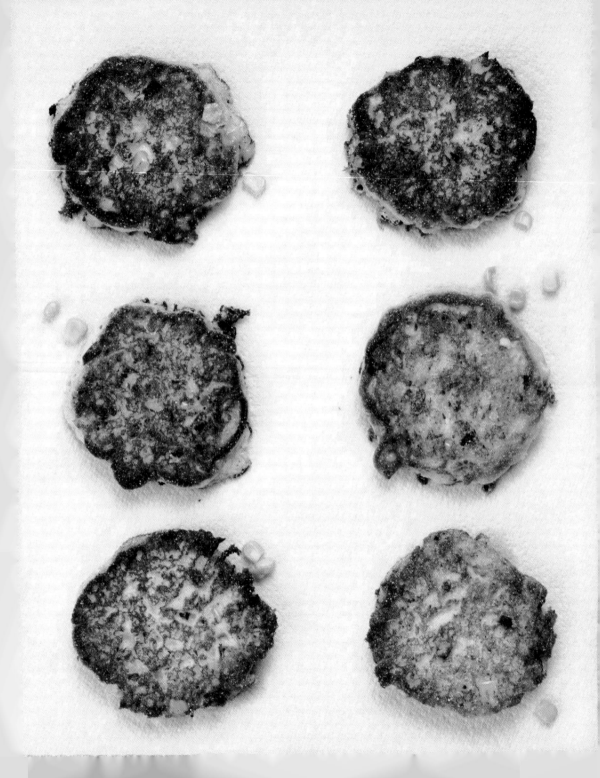

Country Corn Cakes

MAKES: 14 corn cakes

HANDS-ON TIME: 20 min.

TOTAL TIME: 1 hour

- 1 (12-oz.) package frozen whole kernel corn, thawed
- 2 Tbsp. finely chopped onion
- 2 Tbsp. finely chopped celery
- 1 (2-oz.) jar diced pimiento, drained
- 1½ cups buttermilk
- 1 egg, lightly beaten
- 2 Tbsp. butter, melted
- ¼ tsp. table salt
- 1¾ cups self-rising cornmeal mix
- ¼ cup vegetable oil, divided

❶ Finely chop ½ cup corn. Combine chopped and unchopped corn, onion, and next 6 ingredients in a medium bowl; stir well. Gradually add cornmeal, stirring just until moistened.

❷ Heat 2 Tbsp. oil in a large skillet over medium-high heat. Pour ¼ cup batter into skillet for each corn cake, cooking 3 or 4 cakes at a time. Cook 4 to 5 minutes on each side or until browned. Drain cakes on paper towels. Repeat procedure using remaining batter and adding oil to skillet, if necessary. Cool.

shortcut secret

Freeze corn cakes in a labeled airtight container up to 1 month. To reheat, place cakes on ungreased baking sheets. Bake at 350° for 10 to 12 minutes or until thoroughly heated.

Fried Confetti Corn

MAKES: 8 servings
HANDS-ON TIME: 30 min.
TOTAL TIME: 30 min.

Crisp, crumbled bacon puts this irresistible dish over the top.

8 bacon slices
6 cups fresh sweet corn kernels (about 8 ears)
1 cup diced sweet onion
1/2 cup chopped red bell pepper
1/2 cup chopped green bell pepper
1 (8-oz.) package cream cheese, cubed
1/2 cup half-and-half
1 tsp. sugar
1 tsp. table salt
1 tsp. black pepper

❶ Cook bacon in a large skillet over medium-high heat 6 to 8 minutes or until crisp. Remove bacon, and drain on paper towels, reserving 2 Tbsp. drippings in skillet. Coarsely crumble bacon.

❷ Sauté corn and next 3 ingredients in hot drippings in skillet over medium-high heat 6 minutes or until tender. Add cream cheese and half-and-half, stirring until cream cheese melts. Stir in sugar and next 2 ingredients. Transfer to a serving dish, and top with bacon.

make it a meal

Sweet, creamy, and decadently rich, this fried corn would be great nestled next to a piece of fried chicken and a side of greens.

Lela's Hush Puppies

MAKES: 6 to 8 servings

HANDS-ON TIME: 34 min.

TOTAL TIME: 1 hour, 4 min.

- 2¼ cups self-rising white cornmeal mix
- ½ cup chopped green bell pepper
- ½ medium onion, chopped
- 1 tsp. table salt
- ½ tsp. ground black pepper
- ¼ tsp. ground red pepper
- 1 cup buttermilk
- 2 large eggs
- Vegetable oil

❶ Combine first 6 ingredients in a bowl; make a well in center of mixture.

❷ Whisk together buttermilk and eggs; add to dry ingredients, stirring just until moistened. Let mixture stand 30 minutes.

❸ Pour oil to depth of 2 inches in a Dutch oven; heat to 375°.

❹ Drop batter by heaping teaspoonfuls into hot oil. Fry, in batches, 2 minutes on each side or until golden. Drain on wire racks over paper towels; serve hot.

test kitchen note

If you were raised on fried hush puppies made with a mix of all-purpose flour and cornmeal, you'll be pleasantly surprised by the airy texture and bold flavors of this all-cornmeal version.

Okra-and-Corn Maque Choux

MAKES: 4 servings

HANDS-ON TIME: 30 min.

TOTAL TIME: 30 min.

- $1/4$ lb. spicy smoked sausage, diced
- $1/2$ cup chopped sweet onion
- $1/2$ cup chopped green bell pepper
- 2 garlic cloves, minced
- 3 cups fresh corn kernels
- 1 cup sliced fresh okra
- 1 cup peeled, seeded, and diced tomato ($1/2$ lb.)

❶ Sauté sausage in a large skillet over medium-high heat 3 minutes or until browned. Add onion, bell pepper, and garlic, and sauté 5 minutes or until tender. Add corn, okra, and tomato; cook, stirring often, 10 minutes. Add salt and pepper to taste.

NOTE: We tested with Conecuh Original Spicy and Hot Smoked Sausage.

community chat

This was so great and really easy. You could definitely add a little more sausage and serve over rice for a meal! It's also tasty for breakfast the next morning with grits.

3 Tbsp. olive oil
1½ Tbsp. butter
3 lb. small Yukon gold or red potatoes, peeled
¼ cup lemon juice
4 tsp. chopped fresh thyme
¾ tsp. table salt
½ tsp. black pepper

Church-Style Lemon Roasted Potatoes

MAKES: 6 to 8 servings
HANDS-ON TIME: 28 min.
TOTAL TIME: 1 hour, 8 min.

❶ Preheat oven to 400°. Cook oil and butter in a skillet over medium heat, stirring constantly, 3 to 4 minutes or until butter begins to turn golden brown. Remove butter mixture from heat, and add peeled potatoes, tossing gently to coat.

❷ Spread potatoes in a single layer in a 15- x 10-inch jelly-roll pan.

❸ Bake at 400° for 40 to 45 minutes or until potatoes are golden brown and tender, stirring twice. Transfer potatoes to a large serving bowl, and toss with lemon juice, thyme, salt, and pepper until well coated. Serve potatoes immediately.

shortcut secret

If you don't want to peel little potatoes, you can use larger peeled Yukons. Simply cut into large chunks, and bake as directed. Any leftover potatoes are great for potato salad the next day.

Rice Croquettes

MAKES: 1½ dozen

HANDS-ON TIME: 25 min.

TOTAL TIME: 55 min.

Serve these crisp rice bites with your favorite rémoulade sauce.

1⅓ cups extra-long-grain enriched white rice

½ tsp. table salt

1½ cups panko (Japanese breadcrumbs), divided

3 large eggs

1 cup (4 oz.) shredded Parmesan cheese

2 Tbsp. chopped fresh basil

1 tsp. minced garlic

½ tsp. freshly ground black pepper

Vegetable oil

❶ Bring 2⅔ cups water to a boil over medium-high heat; add rice and salt. Cover, reduce heat to low, and simmer 20 minutes or until liquid is absorbed and rice is tender. Cool 10 minutes.

❷ Stir together rice, ½ cup breadcrumbs, and next 5 ingredients.

❸ Shape rice mixture into 18 (¼-cup) balls. Dredge in remaining 1 cup breadcrumbs.

❹ Pour oil to a depth of 3 inches in a Dutch oven. Heat oil to 350° over medium-high heat. Fry rice balls, in batches, 2 to 2½ minutes on each side or until golden brown. Drain.

community chat

Good choice for a quick side. Great with chicken or salmon.

Sautéed Garlic Spinach

MAKES: 4 servings
HANDS-ON TIME: 10 min.
TOTAL TIME: 10 min.

1 garlic clove, pressed
1 tsp. olive oil

1 (10-oz.) bag fresh
   spinach

1 Sauté garlic in hot oil in a nonstick skillet over medium-high heat for 30 seconds. Add spinach; cook 2 to 3 minutes or until spinach is wilted. Add salt and pepper to taste. Serve spinach with a slotted spoon or tongs.

test kitchen note

The secret to sautéing spinach properly is in the timing. Be sure not to overcook it by simply cooking it until it begins to wilt.

Sautéed Squash and Tomatoes

3 thick hickory-smoked bacon slices
1 cup chopped sweet onion
3 garlic cloves, minced
1 Tbsp. chopped fresh thyme
1 tsp. chopped fresh oregano
1 bay leaf
4 cups sliced zucchini
4 cups sliced yellow or zephyr squash
2 cups cherry tomatoes, halved
2 Tbsp. butter
1 Tbsp. red wine vinegar
Garnish: bay leaf

MAKES: 8 to 10 servings
HANDS-ON TIME: 47 min.
TOTAL TIME: 47 min.

❶ Sauté bacon in a large skillet over medium-high heat 8 minutes or until crisp; remove bacon, and drain on paper towels, reserving 2 Tbsp. drippings in skillet. Crumble bacon.

❷ Sauté onion and next 4 ingredients in hot drippings 4 minutes or until onion is tender. Add zucchini and squash; cook, stirring often, 10 minutes. Stir in tomatoes, and cook, stirring occasionally, 10 minutes. Remove from heat, and stir in butter and vinegar. Stir in crumbled bacon. Add salt and pepper to taste. Remove and discard bay leaf.

community chat

This recipe is delicious and a good way to try new squash varieties. Use crumbled bacon as a tasty garnish.

4 lb. yellow squash, sliced

1 large sweet onion, finely chopped

1 cup (4 oz.) shredded Cheddar cheese

1/2 cup chopped fresh chives

1 (8-oz.) container sour cream

1 tsp. garlic salt

1 tsp. freshly ground black pepper

2 large eggs, lightly beaten

2 1/2 cups soft, fresh breadcrumbs, divided

1 1/4 cups (5 oz.) freshly shredded Parmesan cheese, divided

2 Tbsp. butter, melted

Two-Cheese Squash Casserole

MAKES: 10 to 12 servings
HANDS-ON TIME: 25 min.
TOTAL TIME: 1 hour, 8 min.

❶ Preheat oven to 350°. Cook yellow squash and onion in boiling water to cover in a Dutch oven 8 minutes or just until tender; drain squash mixture well.

❷ Combine squash mixture, Cheddar cheese, next 5 ingredients, 1 cup breadcrumbs, and 3/4 cup Parmesan cheese in a large bowl. Spoon into a lightly greased 13- x 9-inch baking dish.

❸ Stir together melted butter and remaining 1 1/2 cups breadcrumbs and 1/2 cup Parmesan cheese. Sprinkle breadcrumb mixture over top of casserole.

❹ Bake at 350° for 35 to 40 minutes or until set.

test kitchen note

For a tasty and colorful twist, substitute sliced zucchini for half of the yellow squash.

Fried Green Tomatoes

MAKES: 6 servings
HANDS-ON TIME: 30 min.
TOTAL TIME: 30 min.

Serve these as fried green tomato sandwiches topped with coleslaw.

1 large egg, lightly beaten
$^1/_2$ cup buttermilk
$^1/_2$ cup self-rising cornmeal mix
$^1/_2$ tsp. table salt
$^1/_2$ tsp. black pepper
$^1/_2$ cup all-purpose flour
3 medium-size, firm green tomatoes, cut into $^1/_3$-inch-thick slices (about 1$^1/_4$ lb.)
Vegetable oil

❶ Whisk together egg and buttermilk. Combine cornmeal mix, salt, pepper, and $^1/_4$ cup flour in a shallow dish. Dredge tomato slices in remaining $^1/_4$ cup flour; dip in egg mixture, and dredge in cornmeal mixture.

❷ Pour oil to a depth of $^1/_2$ inch in a large cast-iron skillet; heat to 375° over medium-high heat. Drop tomatoes, in batches, into hot oil, and cook 2 minutes on each side or until golden. Drain on paper towels. Sprinkle hot tomatoes with salt to taste.

The cornmeal-and-flour crust is what sets this recipe apart from others.

Tipsy Red-and-Yellow Melon Salad gets its name from the marinade that contains vodka and black raspberry liqueur.

Tipsy Red-and-Yellow Melon Salad

MAKES: 6 to 8 servings
HANDS-ON TIME: 20 min.
TOTAL TIME: 1 hour, 20 min.

½ (6-lb.) red watermelon
½ (6-lb.) yellow watermelon
1 cup fresh lemon juice (about 10 to 12 lemons)
⅔ cup sugar
½ cup vodka
⅓ cup black raspberry liqueur
Pinch of fine sea salt
1 Tbsp. chopped fresh mint
Garnish: fresh mint sprigs

❶ Scoop watermelons into balls using various size melon ballers, and place watermelon in a large bowl.

❷ Whisk together lemon juice and next 4 ingredients in a medium bowl until sugar dissolves. Pour lemon juice mixture over watermelon balls; gently stir to coat. Cover and chill 1 to 2 hours.

❸ Gently toss watermelon balls. Sprinkle with chopped fresh mint. Serve immediately with a slotted spoon.

shortcut secret

The quickest way to juice a lemon is to use a mechanical juicer.

5

Soup & Salad Suppers

Skip the deli, and create your own specialties for dinner tonight.

2 (9-oz.) packages refrigerated cheese-filled tortellini

$^1/_2$ cup olive oil

$^1/_2$ cup freshly grated Parmesan cheese

3 Tbsp. fresh lemon juice

2 garlic cloves

1 tsp. table salt

2 cups baby heirloom tomatoes, halved

1 cup fresh corn kernels

$^1/_2$ cup thinly sliced green onions

$^1/_2$ cup coarsely chopped fresh basil

❶ Prepare tortellini according to package directions.

❷ Meanwhile, process olive oil and next 4 ingredients in a blender until smooth. Toss olive oil mixture with hot cooked tortellini, tomatoes, and next 3 ingredients. Season with salt and pepper to taste.

TOP ❺ SOUPS & SALADS

Tortellini-and-Tomato Salad

MAKES: 6 servings

HANDS-ON TIME: 20 min.

TOTAL TIME: 20 min.

community chat

If you only have one package of tortellini, you can add in some bow tie pasta.

TOP 5 · SOUPS & SALADS

Crispy Goat Cheese-Topped Arugula Salad with Pomegranate Vinaigrette

MAKES: 8 servings

HANDS-ON TIME: 25 min.

TOTAL TIME: 1 hour, 50 min., including vinaigrette

test kitchen note

Dip a knife in hot water to get clean slices of cheese.

---

4 (4-oz.) goat cheese logs
$1/2$ cup all-purpose flour
$1/2$ tsp. black pepper
2 egg whites
1 cup panko (Japanese breadcrumbs)
4 Tbsp. olive oil
2 (5-oz.) containers baby arugula
4 large navel oranges, peeled and sectioned
Pomegranate Vinaigrette

❶ Cut each goat cheese log into 6 ($1/2$-inch) slices. Combine flour and black pepper in a shallow dish. Whisk together egg whites and 2 Tbsp. water in another shallow dish. Place panko in a third shallow dish. Dredge goat cheese in flour mixture, dip in egg mixture, and dredge in panko. Arrange goat cheese in a single layer in an aluminum foil-lined jelly-roll pan; cover and chill 30 minutes to 4 hours.

❷ Cook half of goat cheese rounds in 2 Tbsp. hot oil in a large nonstick skillet over medium heat 2 to 3 minutes on each side or until lightly browned. Drain on paper towels. Repeat with remaining oil and goat cheese rounds.

❸ Divide arugula and orange sections among 8 plates; drizzle with Pomegranate Vinaigrette. Top each salad with 3 goat cheese rounds.

Pomegranate Vinaigrette:

MAKES: about $2/3$ cup

HANDS-ON TIME: 20 min.

TOTAL TIME: 55 min.

$1^1/2$ cups pomegranate juice
$1/3$ cup olive oil
5 Tbsp. honey
1 Tbsp. white wine vinegar
1 tsp. Dijon mustard
$1/4$ tsp. freshly ground black pepper
$1/8$ tsp. table salt

Bring pomegranate juice to a boil in a medium saucepan over medium-high heat; reduce heat to medium, and cook, stirring occasionally, 15 minutes or until reduced to $1/4$ cup. Transfer to a small bowl. Cool completely (about 30 minutes). Whisk in oil and next 5 ingredients.

TOP **5** SOUPS & SALADS

Spiced Orange Salad with Goat Cheese and Glazed Pecans

MAKES: 6 servings
HANDS-ON TIME: 20 min.
TOTAL TIME: 20 min.

test kitchen note

This is a favorite first course for holiday dinner parties. We often substitute Gorgonzola for goat cheese and top the oranges with sliced fresh strawberries.

6 large navel oranges
6 cups watercress
$1/4$ cup canola oil
$1/4$ cup rice wine vinegar
2 Tbsp. chopped fresh chives
1 Tbsp. light brown sugar
1 Tbsp. grated fresh ginger
$1/4$ tsp. table salt
$1/2$ cup crumbled goat cheese
1 (3.5-oz.) package roasted glazed pecan pieces

Peel oranges, and cut into $1/4$-inch-thick slices. Arrange watercress on a serving platter; top with orange slices. Whisk together canola oil and next 5 ingredients; drizzle over salad. Sprinkle with goat cheese and pecans.

Refreshing Chilled Strawberry Soup offers a splash of excitement with the addition of Riesling. Serve this spring soup for a first course or as a dessert.

- 3 cups sliced fresh strawberries
- 1 cup plain Greek yogurt
- ¹/₂ cup Riesling
- ¹/₃ cup sugar
- Garnishes: olive oil, freshly ground black pepper, sliced fresh strawberries

Process strawberries and next 3 ingredients in a blender or food processor until smooth, stopping to scrape down sides as needed. Cover and chill 2 hours.

Chilled Strawberry Soup

MAKES: 4 cups

HANDS-ON TIME: 10 min.

TOTAL TIME: 2 hours, 10 min.

shortcut secret

Use a strawberry slicer to quickly cut the strawberry garnish.

6 (6-inch) fajita-size corn tortillas

2 Tbsp. canola oil, divided

2 medium tomatoes, cored and halved

1 onion, chopped

2 garlic cloves

1 (32-oz.) container reduced-sodium fat-free chicken broth

2 cups low-sodium tomato juice

1 bay leaf

$1/4$ tsp. ground cumin

$1/4$ tsp. ground coriander

$1/4$ tsp. ground red pepper

$1^1/2$ lb. skinned and boned chicken breasts, cut into $1/2$-inch-wide strips

4 green onions (white part only), thinly sliced

$1/2$ cup fresh lime juice

$1/4$ cup chopped fresh cilantro

$1/2$ cup crumbled queso fresco (fresh Mexican cheese)

1 medium avocado, chopped

TOP **5** SOUPS & SALADS

Mexican Tomato Soup

MAKES: 4 to 6 servings

HANDS-ON TIME: 1 hour, 5 min.

TOTAL TIME: 1 hour, 40 min.

1 Preheat oven to 400°. Brush 1 side of tortillas with 1 Tbsp. oil; cut tortillas in half. Stack tortilla halves, and cut crosswise into $1/4$-inch-wide strips. Arrange strips in a single layer on a lightly greased baking sheet. Add salt and pepper to taste. Bake at 400° for 15 minutes or until golden, stirring halfway through. Cool.

2 Meanwhile, heat a nonstick skillet over high heat 2 minutes. Add tomato halves, and cook, turning occasionally, 10 minutes or until charred on all sides. (Tomatoes may stick.) Transfer to a food processor. Sauté onion in remaining 1 Tbsp. hot oil in skillet over medium heat 3 to 5 minutes or until tender. Add garlic; sauté 2 minutes or until fragrant. Transfer onion mixture to food processor with tomatoes; process until smooth.

3 Cook tomato mixture in a Dutch oven over medium-high heat, stirring occasionally, 5 minutes or until thickened. Stir in broth and tomato juice. Add bay leaf and next 3 ingredients; bring to a boil. Reduce heat to medium-low, and simmer, partially covered and stirring occasionally, 20 minutes. Add chicken; simmer, stirring occasionally, 5 to 7 minutes or until chicken is done.

4 Discard bay leaf. Stir in green onions and next 2 ingredients. Add salt and pepper to taste. Divide queso fresco among 4 to 6 soup bowls; top with tortilla strips. Ladle soup into bowls. Top with avocado.

test kitchen note

Charring the tomatoes creates a wonderfully smoky flavor to this zesty Mexican Tomato Soup. Adjust the amount of red pepper to your desired level of heat.

Sweet Potato Soup

MAKES: 8 cups

HANDS-ON TIME: 35 min.

TOTAL TIME: 1 hour

2 Tbsp. butter
1 medium onion, chopped
2 garlic cloves, minced
5 1/2 cups reduced-sodium fat-free chicken broth
2 lb. sweet potatoes, peeled and chopped (2 large)

1 cup apple cider
1 tsp. minced canned chipotle pepper in adobo sauce
1 tsp. table salt
2 Tbsp. fresh lime juice
1/2 cup sour cream
2 tsp. fresh lime juice
Garnish: fresh parsley

❶ Melt butter in a large saucepan over medium-high heat; add onion, and sauté 5 to 7 minutes or until tender. Add garlic; sauté 1 minute. Stir in broth and next 4 ingredients. Bring to a boil; reduce heat to medium-low, and simmer 20 minutes or until potatoes are tender.

❷ Process mixture with a handheld blender until smooth. (If you don't have a handheld blender, cool mixture 10 minutes, and process, in batches, in a regular blender until smooth. Return to saucepan, and proceed with Step 3.)

❸ Cook potato mixture over low heat, stirring occasionally, 5 minutes or until thoroughly heated. Stir in 2 Tbsp. lime juice. Whisk together sour cream and 2 tsp. lime juice. Ladle soup into bowls, and drizzle each serving with sour cream mixture. Garnish, if desired.

shortcut secret

Make the soup through Step 2 the day before. Reheat, and stir in the lime juice before serving.

Made with leftover ham, mashed potatoes, sweet peas, and dinner rolls, this comfort food favorite comes together in just 15 minutes.

Loaded Potato Soup

MAKES: 4 to 6 servings
HANDS-ON TIME: 15 min.
TOTAL TIME: 15 min.

2 Tbsp. butter
1 cup diced smoked ham
4 sliced green onions
1 garlic clove, minced
2 cups mashed potatoes
1 (14-oz.) can low-sodium chicken broth
1 cup milk
$^1/_3$ cup sweet peas
2 tsp. chopped fresh thyme
2 cups torn dinner rolls
1 cup (4 oz.) shredded Cheddar cheese

Preheat broiler. Melt butter in a 3-qt. saucepan; add ham, onions, and garlic. Sauté until golden. Stir in potatoes and next 4 ingredients. Bring to a boil; reduce heat. Simmer 8 minutes or until thickened. Add salt and pepper to taste. Spoon into 4 broiler-safe bowls. Top with torn dinner rolls; sprinkle with Cheddar cheese. Place bowls on a baking sheet. Broil 3 minutes or until golden brown.

shortcut secret

Purchase mashed potatoes from the deli for a quick addition to this recipe.

Red Lentil Soup

MAKES: 11 cups

HANDS-ON TIME: 25 min.

TOTAL TIME: 55 min.

2 Tbsp. butter
1 sweet onion, diced
1 cup chopped carrots
1 cup chopped celery
4 garlic cloves, minced
1 (28-oz.) can diced tomatoes
2 cups dried red lentils
2 extra-large chicken bouillon cubes
$1/2$ tsp. ground cumin
$1/2$ tsp. table salt
$1/4$ tsp. black pepper
1 cup chopped fresh basil

1 Melt butter in a Dutch oven over medium-high heat. Add onion and next 3 ingredients; sauté 5 to 6 minutes or until tender. Add tomatoes, next 5 ingredients, and 5 cups water.

2 Bring to a boil; reduce heat to medium, and cook, stirring occasionally, 30 minutes or until lentils are tender. Stir in basil just before serving.

make it a meal

To make a tasty sandwich, layer chutney, Havarti cheese slices, deli pork slices, and Dijon mustard between multigrain bread slices. Spread outside of sandwiches with butter; cook on a hot griddle over medium heat 3 minutes on each side or until lightly browned.

Hoppin' John Soup

MAKES: 11 cups

HANDS-ON TIME: 30 min.

TOTAL TIME: 2 hours, 5 min., not including croutons

- 1/2 (16-oz.) package dried black-eyed peas, rinsed and sorted
- 2 lb. smoked turkey wings
- 1/3 cup finely chopped country ham
- 1/4 tsp. dried crushed red pepper
- 2 garlic cloves, minced
- 1 jalapeño pepper, seeded and minced
- 2 carrots, cut into 1-inch pieces
- 1 celery rib, diced
- 1 large sweet onion, diced
- 1 bay leaf
- 2 Tbsp. canola oil
- 1/2 (16-oz.) package fresh collard greens, trimmed and finely chopped
- 1 Tbsp. hot sauce
- 1 Tbsp. apple cider vinegar
- Hot cooked brown rice
- Cornbread Croutons
- Flat-leaf parsley leaves

1 Bring peas, turkey wings, and 6 cups water to a boil in a large Dutch oven. Cover, reduce heat to medium, and simmer 45 minutes or until peas are tender, skimming any foam from surface. Drain peas, reserving 1 1/4 cups liquid. Remove turkey meat from bones. Chop meat.

2 Sauté ham and next 7 ingredients in hot oil in Dutch oven over medium-high heat 10 minutes or until vegetables are tender. Add peas, reserved 1 1/4 cups liquid, turkey meat, collards, hot sauce, and 6 cups water. Bring to a boil; reduce heat to medium, and simmer, stirring occasionally, 30 minutes. Stir in vinegar. Add salt and pepper to taste. Discard bay leaf. Serve over rice with Cornbread Croutons and parsley.

Cornbread Croutons:

Add 1/2 cup chopped fresh cilantro and 2 seeded and chopped jalapeño peppers to your favorite cornbread recipe. Cut cooked cornbread into 1-inch cubes. Bake at 375° in a lightly greased jelly-roll pan until edges are golden, stirring halfway through. **MAKES:** 6 dozen (if using a 9-inch pan); **HANDS-ON TIME:** 10 min.; **TOTAL TIME:** 10 min.

test kitchen note

Use the cornbread croutons to top your favorite soup or salad.

Roasted Sweet Potato Salad

MAKES: 4 servings
HANDS-ON TIME: 30 min.
TOTAL TIME: 1 hour, 5 min.

Mango, avocado, red bell pepper, and sweet potatoes make a colorful presentation as well as a good-for-you meal.

- 1 (24-oz.) package fresh steam-in-bag petite sweet potatoes
- 1 Tbsp. Caribbean jerk seasoning
- 4 Tbsp. olive oil, divided
- 2 Tbsp. fresh lime juice
- 1/4 tsp. table salt
- 1 (5-oz.) package baby arugula
- 1 mango, peeled and diced
- 1 avocado, halved and thinly sliced
- 1/2 red bell pepper, sliced
- 1/2 small red onion, sliced
- 1/2 cup torn fresh basil

1 Preheat oven to 425°. Cut potatoes in half lengthwise; toss with jerk seasoning and 1 Tbsp. oil. Arrange, cut sides down, in a single layer on a lightly greased baking sheet. Bake at 425° for 15 minutes; turn and bake 8 to 10 minutes or until tender. Cool on a wire rack 20 minutes.

2 Whisk together lime juice, salt, and remaining 3 Tbsp. oil in a large bowl. Add arugula and next 5 ingredients, and toss to coat. Arrange on a platter; top with potatoes.

shortcut secret

Use a vegetable peeler rather than a paring knife to peel a mango even faster.

Spring Garden Strawberry Salad

1½ cups trimmed fresh sugar snap peas (about 5 oz.)

1 (4-oz.) package baby arugula

2 cups sliced fresh strawberries

1 cup seeded and chopped English cucumber

¾ cup frozen baby English peas, thawed

4 oz. Gorgonzola cheese, crumbled

6 cooked bacon slices, coarsely chopped

Sweet Basil Vinaigrette

MAKES: 6 servings
HANDS-ON TIME: 30 min.
TOTAL TIME: 40 min., including vinaigrette

❶ Arrange sugar snap peas in a steamer basket over boiling water. Cover; steam 1 to 2 minutes or until crisp-tender. Plunge peas into ice water to stop the cooking process; drain. Cut peas diagonally in half.

❷ Toss together arugula, next 5 ingredients, and sugar snap peas on a large serving platter. Serve with Sweet Basil Vinaigrette.

Sweet Basil Vinaigrette:

MAKES: about 1½ cups
HANDS-ON TIME: 10 min.
TOTAL TIME: 10 min.

⅓ cup red wine vinegar

2 shallots, chopped

3 Tbsp. sugar

3 Tbsp. chopped fresh basil

1 Tbsp. fresh lemon juice

2 tsp. Dijon mustard

¾ tsp. freshly ground black pepper

½ tsp. table salt

¾ cup canola oil

Process first 8 ingredients in a blender until smooth. With blender running, add canola oil in a slow, steady stream, processing until smooth.

community chat

Great spring salad! The Sweet Basil Vinaigrette is worth making instead of using something storebought.

Blueberry Fields Salad

MAKES: 8 servings
HANDS-ON TIME: 20 min.
TOTAL TIME: 20 min.

This is a very tasty and healthy salad. It goes together fast. You could omit the blue cheese (if you don't like it) and still have a delicious salad. It's perfect for company.

$^1/_2$ cup balsamic vinegar
$^1/_3$ cup blueberry preserves
$^1/_3$ cup olive oil
2 (5.5-oz.) packages spring greens and baby spinach mix
2 cups fresh blueberries
1 cup toasted chopped walnuts
1 small red onion, halved and sliced
1 cup crumbled blue cheese

❶ Whisk together vinegar, next 2 ingredients, and salt and freshly ground black pepper to taste in a small bowl.

❷ Combine spinach mix, and next 4 ingredients in a large bowl. Drizzle with desired amount of vinaigrette, and toss to combine. Serve immediately with remaining vinaigrette.

Experience the fresh flavors of spring greens and baby spinach with fresh blueberries, red onion, and tangy blue cheese.

Let the flavor of fresh figs shine in Marinated Fig Salad. An added bonus: This fig salad comes together in just a few minutes.

Marinated Fig Salad

MAKES: 4 servings

HANDS-ON TIME: 15 min.

TOTAL TIME: 45 min.

¼ cup extra virgin olive oil

3 Tbsp. balsamic vinegar

1 Tbsp. honey

1 tsp. coarse-grained Dijon mustard

16 fresh figs, halved

1 (8-oz.) package fresh mozzarella cheese slices

4 oz. thinly sliced Serrano ham or prosciutto, torn into strips

2 cups loosely packed arugula

❶ Whisk together first 4 ingredients and salt and pepper to taste in a medium bowl. Stir in figs; let stand 30 minutes.

❷ Arrange mozzarella and ham on 4 salad plates or a large platter. Spoon fig mixture over cheese and ham. Sprinkle with arugula, and season with salt and pepper to taste.

shortcut secret

Use kitchen shears to quickly cut prosciutto into small strips.

6 artisan bread slices, halved

2 Tbsp. extra virgin olive oil

1 tsp. kosher salt, divided

1 tsp. freshly ground black pepper, divided

6 thick applewood-smoked bacon slices, chopped

1 sweet onion, halved and sliced

1 garlic clove

1/2 cup mayonnaise

2 Tbsp. fresh lemon juice

1 lb. assorted heirloom tomatoes, cut into wedges

1 (5-oz.) package arugula

BLT Salad

MAKES: 4 servings

HANDS-ON TIME: 30 min.

TOTAL TIME: 40 min.

❶ Preheat oven to 400°. Drizzle bread with oil; sprinkle with 1/2 tsp. each kosher salt and black pepper. Bake bread at 400° in a single layer in a jelly-roll pan 12 minutes or until golden.

❷ Cook bacon in a skillet over medium heat, stirring occasionally, 10 minutes or until crisp. Drain on paper towels; reserve 1 Tbsp. drippings in skillet.

❸ Sauté onion in hot drippings over medium-low heat 3 to 5 minutes or until tender.

❹ Smash garlic clove to make a paste. Whisk together mayonnaise, lemon juice, garlic paste, and remaining 1/2 tsp. each kosher salt and black pepper.

❺ Toss together tomatoes, arugula, bacon, onion, and salt and pepper to taste in a large bowl. Pour mayonnaise mixture over tomato mixture, and toss to coat. Serve immediately with toasted bread.

make it a meal

Serve buttered toast or French bread alongside this refreshing main-dish salad.

Three Sisters Salad

MAKES: 8 to 10 servings

HANDS-ON TIME: 20 min.

TOTAL TIME: 3 hours, 10 min., including vinaigrette

This salad brings together the bounty of the summer garden and a combination of fabulous flavors.

2 lb. butternut squash
2 Tbsp. olive oil
1 (15.5-oz.) can cannellini beans, drained and rinsed
2 cups fresh corn kernels
$^1/_2$ small red onion, sliced
$^1/_2$ cup chopped fresh basil
Balsamic Vinaigrette
3 cups loosely packed arugula

❶ Preheat oven to 400°. Peel and seed butternut squash; cut into $^3/_4$-inch cubes. Toss squash with oil to coat; place in a single layer in a lightly greased aluminum foil-lined 15- x 10-inch jelly-roll pan. Bake at 400° for 20 minutes or until squash is just tender and begins to brown (do not overcook), stirring once after 10 minutes. Cool completely (about 20 minutes).

❷ Toss together beans, next 4 ingredients, and squash in a large bowl; cover and chill 2 to 4 hours. Toss with arugula just before serving.

Balsamic Vinaigrette:

Whisk together 2 Tbsp. balsamic vinegar; 1 large shallot, minced; 1 tsp. minced garlic; $^1/_2$ Tbsp. light brown sugar; $^1/_4$ tsp. salt; and $^1/_4$ tsp. seasoned pepper. Gradually add $^1/_4$ cup canola oil in a slow, steady stream, whisking until blended.

community chat

The combination of flavors is fabulous. Purchase precut butternut squash to make it easier, and microwave fresh ears of corn. Everything about this salad is great.

- 8 oz. haricots verts (thin green beans), trimmed
- 1 (5-oz.) package gourmet mixed salad greens
- 2 red Bartlett pears, cut into thin strips
- 1/2 small red onion, sliced
- 4 oz. Gorgonzola cheese, crumbled
- 1 cup Sweet-and-Spicy Pecans
- Sorghum Vinaigrette

Cook beans in boiling salted water to cover 3 to 4 minutes or until crisp-tender; drain. Plunge beans into ice water to stop the cooking process; drain. Toss together salad greens, next 4 ingredients, and beans. Serve with Sorghum Vinaigrette.

Sweet-and-Spicy Pecans

MAKES: about 2 cups
HANDS-ON TIME: 10 min.
TOTAL TIME: 55 min.

- 1/4 cup sorghum syrup
- 2 Tbsp. Demerara sugar
- 1/2 tsp. kosher salt
- 1/4 tsp. ground red pepper
- 2 cups pecan halves
- Parchment paper

1 Preheat oven to 350°. Stir together first 4 ingredients. Add pecan halves; stir until coated. Line a jelly-roll pan with parchment paper, and lightly grease paper. Spread pecans in a single layer in pan.

2 Bake at 350° for 15 minutes or until glaze bubbles slowly and thickens, stirring once after 8 minutes. Transfer pan to a wire rack. Separate pecans into individual pieces; cool completely in pan. If cooled pecans are not crisp, bake 5 more minutes.

Sorghum Vinaigrette

MAKES: about 2 cups
HANDS-ON TIME: 5 min.
TOTAL TIME: 5 min.

- 1/2 cup sorghum syrup
- 1/2 cup malt or apple cider vinegar
- 3 Tbsp. bourbon
- 2 tsp. grated onion
- 1 tsp. salt
- 1 tsp. freshly ground black pepper
- 1/2 tsp. hot sauce
- 1 cup olive oil

Whisk together first 7 ingredients until blended. Add oil in a slow, steady stream, whisking until smooth.

Fresh Pear-and-Green Bean Salad with Sorghum Vinaigrette

MAKES: 8 servings
HANDS-ON TIME: 15 min.
TOTAL TIME: 1 hour, 15 min.

shortcut secret

The Sweet-and-Spicy Pecans are worth the time and effort, but if you are short on time, just toast the pecans instead.

Hearts of Palm-and-Jicama Salad

MAKES: 6 to 8 servings
HANDS-ON TIME: 20 min.
TOTAL TIME: 1 hour, 20 min.

1 (14.4-oz.) can hearts of palm, drained and rinsed

$^1/_4$ red onion, thinly sliced

1 yellow bell pepper, diced

1 jicama, peeled and cut into $^1/_8$-inch strips

1 jalapeño pepper, seeded and minced

$^1/_4$ cup chopped fresh cilantro

$^1/_4$ cup fresh lime juice

$^1/_4$ cup fresh orange juice

2 Tbsp. olive oil

1 tsp. table salt

$^1/_2$ tsp. ground cumin

1 avocado, diced

Cut hearts of palm crosswise into $^1/_2$-inch slices. Stir together hearts of palm and next 10 ingredients in a large bowl. Cover and chill 1 to 8 hours. Stir in avocado just before serving.

test kitchen note

Pick a jicama that's about the size of a large grapefruit, and use a vegetable peeler to remove the skin.

Lemony olive bread croutons top this lightly dressed salad. Double the dressing, if desired.

Herbs-and-Greens Salad

MAKES: 6 to 8 servings
HANDS-ON TIME: 10 min.
TOTAL TIME: 30 min.

½ tsp. lemon zest
4 Tbsp. olive oil, divided
3 cups 1-inch olive bread cubes*
4 cups torn butter lettuce (about 1 head)
2 cups firmly packed fresh baby spinach

1 cup torn escarole
½ cup loosely packed fresh parsley leaves
¼ cup fresh 1-inch chive pieces
2 Tbsp. fresh lemon juice

1 Preheat oven to 425°. Stir together lemon zest and 1 Tbsp. olive oil in a large bowl. Add bread cubes, and toss to coat. Arrange in a single layer on a baking sheet. Bake at 425° for 5 minutes or until crisp. Cool completely (about 15 minutes).

2 Meanwhile, combine butter lettuce and next 4 ingredients in a large bowl. Drizzle with lemon juice and remaining 3 Tbsp. olive oil, and toss to coat. Add salt and pepper to taste. Serve immediately with toasted bread cubes.

* Ciabatta, focaccia, or country white bread may be substituted.

shortcut secret

Prep, bake, and cool the croutons up to three days ahead, and store in an airtight container.

Warm Lentil-and-Potato Salad

MAKES: 8 servings

HANDS-ON TIME: 25 min.

TOTAL TIME: 50 min.

French green lentils add flavorful texture. They remain firm after cooking, while traditional brown lentils turn soft.

$^1/_2$ cup dried French green lentils

1 (28-oz.) package small red potatoes, halved

5 bacon slices

3 Tbsp. olive oil

2 large shallots, finely chopped

1 celery rib, sliced

2 garlic cloves

2 to 3 Tbsp. red wine vinegar

2 tsp. whole grain Dijon mustard

$1^1/_2$ cups loosely packed fresh flat-leaf parsley leaves

❶ Bring lentils and 4 cups salted water to a boil in a heavy 2-qt. saucepan over medium-high heat. Reduce heat to low; simmer 20 to 25 minutes or just until tender.

❷ Meanwhile, cook potatoes in boiling salted water to cover 15 minutes or just until tender. Drain lentils and potatoes.

❸ Cook bacon in a large, deep nonstick skillet over medium heat 6 to 7 minutes or until crisp; remove bacon, and drain on paper towels, reserving 2 Tbsp. drippings in skillet. Crumble bacon.

❹ Add olive oil to hot drippings in skillet, and heat over medium heat. Sauté shallots, celery, and garlic in hot olive oil mixture 3 minutes. Remove from heat, and stir in vinegar and mustard. Add salt and pepper to taste. Gently stir in lentils, potatoes, bacon, and parsley.

community chat

Extremely good! This recipe is a keeper. Great for the family and when company is coming for dinner. Comfort food without the guilt! And no mayo—fabulous.

Simple Beet Salad

MAKES: 6 to 8 servings
HANDS-ON TIME: 20 min.
TOTAL TIME: 2 hours, 13 min.

2 lb. medium beets
$^1/_3$ cup bottled balsamic vinaigrette
$^1/_2$ cup toasted chopped walnuts
Garnish: fresh parsley leaves

❶ Preheat oven to 400°. Divide beets between 2 large pieces of heavy-duty aluminum foil; drizzle with balsamic vinaigrette, and sprinkle with salt and pepper to taste. Seal foil, making 2 loose packets.

❷ Bake at 400° for 45 to 55 minutes until fork-tender.

❸ Cool 1 hour in packets, reserving accumulated liquid.

❹ Peel beets, and cut into slices or wedges. Arrange beets on a serving platter or in a bowl. Drizzle with reserved liquid, and sprinkle with walnuts. Garnish, if desired.

make it a meal

Colorful ingredients and easy preparation deliver delicious dividends. Use a variety of red and yellow beets to add visual appeal.

4 lb. assorted heirloom tomatoes

2 small Kirby cucumbers, sliced

1 small red onion, halved and sliced

Lady Pea Salsa

Fresh basil leaves

Cut tomatoes into wedges or in half, depending on size. Gently toss tomatoes with cucumbers and onion. Top with Lady Pea Salsa and basil.

Lady Pea Salsa

MAKES: about 4 cups
HANDS-ON TIME: 20 min.
TOTAL TIME: 35 min.

1 cup diced unpeeled nectarine

2 jalapeño peppers, seeded and minced

1 Tbsp. sugar

3 Tbsp. fresh lime juice

2 tsp. orange zest

2 tsp. grated fresh ginger

2 cups cooked fresh lady peas

$\frac{1}{2}$ cup chopped fresh cilantro

$\frac{1}{3}$ cup diced red onion

Stir together first 6 ingredients in a large bowl; let stand 15 minutes. Add peas and next 2 ingredients, and gently toss to coat. Serve immediately, or cover and chill up to 24 hours.

Heirloom Tomato Salad

MAKES: 8 servings

HANDS-ON TIME: 15 min.

TOTAL TIME: 50 min.
including pea salsa

shortcut secret

Use a spoon to quickly scoop out the cucumber seeds if you prefer them seedless.

6

Slow-Cooker Surprises

Beat the hectic weeknight rush with meals that practically cook themselves.

1 lb. lean ground beef

1 lb. ground pork sausage

2 tsp. Cajun seasoning

2 (8-oz.) containers refrigerated prechopped celery, onion, and bell pepper mix

2 cups uncooked converted long-grain rice

1/4 tsp. ground red pepper

1 (10-oz.) can diced tomatoes with green chiles, undrained

1 cup chicken broth

TOP **5** SLOW COOKER

Cajun Dirty Rice

MAKES: 8 servings

HANDS-ON TIME: 10 min.

TOTAL TIME: 2 hours, 10 min.

❶ Brown first 3 ingredients in a large skillet over medium-high heat, stirring often, 8 minutes or until meat crumbles and is no longer pink. Transfer mixture to a 5-qt. slow cooker using a slotted spoon.

❷ Stir in celery mix and remaining ingredients. Cover and cook on LOW 2 hours or until liquid is absorbed and rice is tender.

test kitchen note

Rice can be prepared successfully in the slow cooker if you use the right type. Use converted rice because its firmer grain can stand up to the longer cooking time without becoming gummy.

TOP 5 SLOW COOKER

Orange-Molasses BBQ Ribs

MAKES: 6 servings

HANDS-ON TIME: 20 min.

TOTAL TIME: 8 hours, 30 min.

Vegetable cooking spray

2 slabs pork baby back ribs (about 5 lb.), cut in half

1 cup barbecue sauce

¼ cup molasses

¼ cup frozen orange juice concentrate, thawed

2 tsp. hot sauce

1 tsp. jarred minced garlic

¼ tsp. table salt

Garnish: orange slices

❶ Preheat broiler with oven rack 5½ inches from heat. Coat the rack of a broiler pan and broiler pan with cooking spray. Place ribs on rack in broiler pan. Broil 10 minutes.

❷ Meanwhile, stir together barbecue sauce and next 5 ingredients in a medium bowl.

❸ Arrange ribs in a 6-qt. oval slow cooker. Pour sauce over ribs.

❹ Cover and cook on LOW 8 hours. Transfer ribs to a serving platter. Skim fat from juices in slow cooker. Pour juices into a 2-qt. saucepan. Cook over medium-high heat 10 minutes or until reduced to 1½ cups, stirring occasionally. Serve sauce with ribs.

test kitchen note

Browning the ribs in the oven renders water and excess fat, making the sauce thicker.

Save a little money, and skip the Mexican restaurant in favor of a homemade meal.

TOP **5** SLOW COOKER

Beef and Chicken Fajitas

MAKES: 10 servings

HANDS-ON TIME: 15 min.

TOTAL TIME: 7 hours, 15 min.

1½ lb. flat-iron steak, cut into strips
1 lb. skinned and boned chicken breasts, cut into strips
1 tsp. table salt
1 tsp. black pepper
1½ Tbsp. fajita seasoning, divided
4 Tbsp. olive oil, divided
3 Tbsp. fresh lime juice
2 Tbsp. Worcestershire sauce
5 large garlic cloves, minced
1½ (1-lb.) packages frozen pepper stir-fry
10 (8-inch) flour tortillas, warmed
Lime wedges (optional)
Toppings: guacamole, shredded lettuce, chopped tomato, shredded Cheddar cheese

1 Place steak and chicken strips on separate plates; sprinkle with salt, black pepper, and 1 Tbsp. fajita seasoning.

2 Heat 1 Tbsp. oil in an extra-large skillet over medium-high heat. Add steak to pan; cook 3 minutes or until browned, turning once. Place steak in a 5- or 6-qt. slow cooker. Add chicken to pan; cook over medium-high heat 3 minutes or until browned, stirring once. Add chicken to steak in slow cooker.

3 Stir together remaining 3 Tbsp. oil, lime juice, Worcestershire sauce, garlic, and remaining 1½ tsp. fajita seasoning in a medium bowl; pour over chicken and steak in slow cooker. Cover and cook on LOW 5 hours or until meat is tender. Stir in frozen pepper stir-fry. Cover and cook 1 to 2 more hours.

4 Spoon filling into tortillas and, if desired, squeeze lime wedges over filling. Serve with desired toppings.

test kitchen note

Slicing the steak perpendicular against the grain with a sharp, serrated meat knife makes cutting faster.

TOP **5** SLOW COOKER

Steak Soup

MAKES: 6 servings
HANDS-ON TIME: 15 min.
TOTAL TIME: 8 hours, 45 min.

test kitchen note

Sirloin tip is a leaner cut than traditional chuck roast. It yields a very tender "fall apart" texture after the low, slow cooking.

2¼ lb. sirloin tip roast, cut into 1-inch cubes
¼ cup all-purpose flour
½ tsp. table salt
½ tsp. coarsely ground black pepper
2 Tbsp. canola oil
1 (1-oz.) envelope dry onion soup mix
4 cups beef broth
1 Tbsp. tomato paste
1 Tbsp. Worcestershire sauce
2 cups uncooked wide egg noodles

❶ Combine first 4 ingredients in a large zip-top plastic freezer bag; seal bag, and shake to coat beef.

❷ Sauté beef in hot oil in a Dutch oven over medium-high heat 6 minutes or until browned. Place in a 4-qt. slow cooker. Sprinkle onion soup mix over beef. Whisk together broth, tomato paste, and Worcestershire; pour over beef. Cover and cook on LOW 8 hours or until beef is tender.

❸ Add noodles to slow cooker; cover and cook 30 minutes or until noodles are done.

1/4 cup butter
1 large onion, chopped
1/4 cup all-purpose flour
1 (12-oz.) can evaporated milk
1 (32-oz.) container chicken broth
1/4 tsp. table salt
1/2 tsp. freshly ground black pepper
1 (14-oz.) package frozen baby broccoli florets

1 (8-oz.) package pasteurized prepared cheese product, cubed
1 1/2 cups (6 oz.) shredded extra-sharp Cheddar cheese
1 cup (4 oz.) shredded Parmesan cheese
Garnish: additional shredded extra-sharp Cheddar cheese

Three-Cheese Broccoli Soup

MAKES: 8 servings
HANDS-ON TIME: 15 min.
TOTAL TIME: 4 hours, 15 min.

1 Melt butter in a large skillet over medium-high heat. Add onion. Sauté 4 minutes or until tender. Stir in flour. Cook, stirring constantly, 1 minute. Gradually stir in milk until smooth. Pour milk mixture into a lightly greased 4-qt. slow cooker. Stir in broth and next 3 ingredients. Cover and cook on LOW 4 hours or until bubbly.

2 Add cheese cubes, stirring until cubes melt. Add Cheddar cheese and Parmesan cheese, stirring until cheeses melt. Serve immediately.

make it a meal

Serve this tasty soup with ham sandwiches or French bread and mixed salad greens for a delicious weeknight meal.

Grillades and Cheese Grits

MAKES: 6 servings
HANDS-ON TIME: 15 min.
TOTAL TIME: 6 hours, 30 min.

- 2 lb. top round steak (about 1/2 inch thick)
- 1 tsp. table salt, divided
- 1/4 tsp. black pepper
- 1/4 cup all-purpose flour, divided
- 2 Tbsp. vegetable oil
- 2 (8-oz.) containers refrigerated prechopped celery, onion, and bell pepper mix
- 3 garlic cloves, minced
- 1 (14-oz.) can beef broth
- 1 tsp. dried Italian seasoning
- 1/2 tsp. ground red pepper
- 2 (14.5-oz.) cans diced tomatoes with basil, garlic, and oregano
- 2 cups uncooked quick-cooking grits
- 2 cups Gruyère cheese, shredded
- Garnish: chopped fresh parsley

❶ Sprinkle steak with 1/2 tsp. salt and pepper. Set aside 1 Tbsp. flour. Cut steak into 2-inch pieces; dredge in remaining flour.

❷ Heat oil in a large nonstick skillet over medium-high heat; add steak, and cook 3 minutes on each side or until browned. Transfer to a 5-qt. slow cooker. Add celery mix and garlic to skillet; sauté 3 minutes. Add beef broth, stirring to loosen browned bits from bottom of skillet. Stir in Italian seasoning and red pepper. Pour mixture over steak. Drain 1 can tomatoes. Add drained tomatoes and remaining can tomatoes to steak mixture. Cover and cook on LOW 6 hours or until steak is very tender.

❸ Increase heat to HIGH. Stir together reserved flour and 2 Tbsp. water until smooth; gently stir into steak mixture. Cover and cook 15 minutes or until mixture is slightly thickened.

❹ Meanwhile, bring 8 cups water and remaining 1/2 tsp. salt to a boil in a 4-qt. saucepan; gradually whisk in grits. Reduce heat, and simmer, whisking often, 5 minutes or until thickened; stir in cheese. Serve grillades over grits. Garnish, if desired.

make it a meal

Serve this deep South favorite with crusty French bread and a mixed green salad.

Beef Ragu
with Penne

MAKES: 4 servings
HANDS-ON TIME: 8 min.
TOTAL TIME: 4 hours, 8 min.

test kitchen note

You can substitute gemelli, cellentani, or macaroni for the penne.

1 large onion, chopped
2 lb. ground beef
2 (28-oz.) cans crushed tomatoes
1 tsp. kosher salt
1 (16-oz.) package penne pasta
$^1/_4$ cup finely grated Parmesan cheese
2 Tbsp. chopped fresh basil
Freshly ground black pepper

❶ Place onion in a 5-qt. slow cooker. Crumble ground beef over onion, and add tomatoes. Cover and cook on HIGH 4 hours or on LOW 8 hours. Break up any large pieces of beef with a wooden spoon. Add salt. Remove half of sauce, and reserve for another use; keep remaining sauce warm in slow cooker.

❷ Cook pasta according to package directions, stirring often. Drain and transfer to 4 shallow bowls. Spoon meat sauce over each portion of pasta. Serve with Parmesan cheese, basil, and freshly ground black pepper to taste.

1 lb. ground round
1 cup refrigerated
   prechopped onion
2 garlic cloves, minced
   (optional)
1 (24-oz.) jar pasta
   sauce

1 (25-oz.) package
   frozen cheese-filled
   ravioli (do not thaw)
1 (8-oz.) package
   shredded Italian
   six-cheese blend

Shortcut Ravioli Lasagna

MAKES: 4 to 6 servings
HANDS-ON TIME: 15 min.
TOTAL TIME: 6 hours, 15 min.

1 Cook ground round, onion, and, if desired, garlic in a large skillet over medium-high heat until beef crumbles and is no longer pink. Drain, if needed.

2 Spoon ³/₄ cup pasta sauce into bottom of a lightly greased 4-qt. slow cooker. Layer half of ravioli, half of meat mixture, and 1 cup cheese over sauce. Repeat layers with ³/₄ cup sauce, remaining ravioli, and remaining meat mixture. Top with remaining sauce; sprinkle with remaining 1 cup cheese.

3 Cover and cook on LOW 6 hours or until pasta is tender.

shortcut secret

Use your favorite pasta sauce for this ultra-easy dish. We liked the flavor of Newman's Own.

Game-Day Chili

MAKES: 8 servings

HANDS-ON TIME: 14 min.

TOTAL TIME: 4 hours, 14 min.

$3^{1}/_{4}$ lb. ground chuck

1 medium-size green bell pepper, chopped

3 ($14^{1}/_{2}$-oz.) cans diced tomatoes with garlic and onion, undrained

3 ($10^{3}/_{4}$-oz.) cans tomato soup

1 (16-oz.) can light red kidney beans, drained and rinsed

1 (6-oz.) can tomato paste

5 Tbsp. chili powder

1 tsp. freshly ground black pepper

$^{1}/_{2}$ tsp. paprika

Toppings: sour cream, shredded Cheddar cheese, chopped green onions, sliced black olives, corn chips

❶ Cook meat in a large nonstick skillet over medium-high heat 12 to 14 minutes or until meat crumbles and is no longer pink; drain.

❷ Place meat in a 5- or 6-qt. slow cooker; stir in $^{1}/_{2}$ cup water, bell pepper, and next 7 ingredients. Cover and cook on HIGH 4 hours. Serve with desired toppings.

shortcut secret

Freeze any leftovers for a great make-ahead comfort dish.

French Dip Sandwiches

MAKES: 12 servings

HANDS-ON TIME: 5 min.

TOTAL TIME: 7 hours, 5 min.

Feel free to substitute smaller rolls to make bite-size sandwiches, if desired.

1 (3½- to 4-lb.) boneless chuck roast, trimmed and cut in half

½ cup soy sauce

1 beef bouillon cube

1 bay leaf

3 to 4 peppercorns, crushed

1 tsp. dried rosemary, crushed

1 tsp. dried thyme

1 tsp. garlic powder

12 French sandwich rolls, split

❶ Place roast in a 5-qt. slow cooker. Combine soy sauce and next 6 ingredients; pour over roast. Add water to slow cooker until roast is almost covered.

❷ Cover and cook on LOW 7 hours or until very tender. Remove roast, reserving broth; shred roast with 2 forks. Divide shredded meat evenly among rolls, and serve with reserved broth for dipping.

make it a meal

Serve with sweet potato fries and coleslaw for a quick weeknight supper.

Easy Burritos

MAKES: 8 to 10 servings

HANDS-ON TIME: 30 min.

TOTAL TIME: 8 hours, 42 min., including Pico de Gallo

1 large onion, sliced into rings

1 (3- to 4-lb.) sirloin beef roast

1 (1-oz.) package taco seasoning mix

16 (6-inch) fajita-size flour tortillas

4 cups (16 oz.) shredded Cheddar or Monterey Jack cheese

Toppings: diced tomatoes, diced onions, sliced jalapeño peppers, sour cream, black beans

Pico de Gallo

❶ Place onion in a 5-qt. slow cooker; add roast and ¹/₂ cup water. Sprinkle taco seasoning mix over top of roast.

❷ Cover and cook on LOW 8 hours. Remove roast; shred with 2 forks.

❸ Heat tortillas according to package directions. Using a slotted spoon, spoon beef mixture down centers of tortillas; top with cheese and desired toppings, and roll up. Serve with Pico de Gallo.

Pico de Gallo

MAKES: 3 cups

HANDS-ON TIME: 12 min.

TOTAL TIME: 12 min.

3 cups diced plum tomatoes

¹/₂ cup diced red onion

¹/₃ cup chopped fresh cilantro

¹/₄ to ¹/₃ cup diced jalapeño peppers

¹/₃ cup fresh lime juice

¹/₂ tsp. olive oil

¹/₄ tsp. table salt

¹/₄ tsp. black pepper

Stir together all ingredients in a medium bowl. Cover and chill until ready to serve.

community chat

This meal was so simple to make—your family will love it!

Louisiana-Style Smothered Pork Chops

MAKES: 4 servings

HANDS-ON TIME: 15 min.

TOTAL TIME: 6 hours, 25 min.

4 oz. smoked sausage, chopped
3 Tbsp. all-purpose flour
1 tsp. table salt
$^1/_2$ tsp. black pepper
4 (1$^1/_4$-inch-thick) bone-in center-cut pork chops
3 Tbsp. vegetable oil
1 (16-oz.) package frozen gumbo vegetable mix
1 (14-oz.) can chicken broth
$^1/_2$ tsp. dried thyme
1 Tbsp. cornstarch
Hot cooked rice
4 green onions, sliced
Hot sauce (optional)

❶ Sauté sausage in a large skillet over medium-high heat until browned. Drain sausage, reserving drippings in pan.

❷ Combine flour, salt, and black pepper in a large zip-top plastic freezer bag; add pork chops. Seal bag, and shake to coat.

❸ Add oil to drippings in skillet. Cook pork chops in hot oil over medium-high heat 3 minutes on each side or until browned. Transfer pork chops to a 5- or 6-qt. slow cooker. Layer vegetables and sausage over pork chops; add broth and thyme. Cover and cook on LOW 6 hours.

❹ Remove pork chops from slow cooker; cover and keep warm. Increase temperature to HIGH. Combine cornstarch and 2 Tbsp. water, stirring until smooth. Stir cornstarch mixture into vegetables in slow cooker. Cook, uncovered, 10 minutes or until thickened.

❺ Spoon rice onto serving plates; top with pork chops. Spoon vegetables and sauce over pork chops. Sprinkle vegetables with green onions, and serve with hot sauce, if desired.

make it a meal

Serve this tasty dish with rice and crusty French bread.

Pork Carnitas Nachos

MAKES: 4 servings
HANDS-ON TIME: 10 min.
TOTAL TIME: 6 hours, 10 min.

1 onion, sliced
2 Tbsp. chopped canned chipotle peppers in adobo sauce or 2 fresh jalapeño peppers, seeded and sliced
2- to 3-lb. boned pork butt or shoulder
4 garlic cloves, slivered
1 Tbsp. vegetable oil
Tortilla chips
Toppings: sliced jalapeño peppers, shredded Monterey Jack cheese, salsa verde, fresh salsa

❶ Combine onion, peppers, and ¼ cup water in a 5-qt. slow cooker. Using a knife, make slits all over pork, and insert garlic into slits. Add salt and pepper to taste. Heat a large Dutch oven over medium-high heat; add oil. Brown roast on all sides, about 8 minutes. Transfer roast to slow cooker. Pour ½ cup water into Dutch oven; stir over low heat with a wooden spoon to loosen browned bits from bottom of Dutch oven. Pour liquid into slow cooker. Cover and cook on HIGH 6 hours.

❷ Remove roast from slow cooker; cool. Shred pork using 2 forks. Return pulled pork to slow cooker, stirring to combine. Serve pork over tortilla chips with desired toppings.

community chat

If there are leftovers, you can freeze the pork for a quick meal later.

Sweet 'n' Spicy Braised Pork Tacos

MAKES: 8 to 10 servings
HANDS-ON TIME: 7 min.
TOTAL TIME: 10 hours, 17 min.

- 3 lb. boneless pork shoulder roast (Boston butt)
- 1/2 tsp. table salt
- 1/2 tsp. freshly ground black pepper
- 1 Tbsp. vegetable oil
- 2 (14 1/2-oz.) cans diced tomatoes with garlic and onion
- 1 medium-size sweet onion, chopped
- 1 to 2 canned chipotle peppers in adobo sauce, chopped
- 2 Tbsp. apple cider vinegar
- 2 Tbsp. dark brown sugar
- 1/4 tsp. ground cumin
- 6 cups cooked white rice
- 1 (15-oz.) can black beans
- 16 to 20 (6-inch) fajita-size flour tortillas, warmed
- Garnishes: fresh cilantro sprigs, lime wedges

1 Sprinkle pork with salt and pepper. Cook pork in hot oil in a large skillet over medium-high heat 2 to 3 minutes on all sides or until pork is browned. Stir together tomatoes and next 5 ingredients in a 5-qt. slow cooker. Add pork, turning to coat.

2 Cover and cook on LOW 10 hours or until pork is fork-tender. Transfer pork to a cutting board, and let stand 10 minutes. Shred pork with 2 forks. Return shredded pork to slow cooker, and stir until blended. Add salt and pepper to taste. Serve immediately with a slotted spoon over rice and black beans in tortillas.

shortcut secret

To quickly warm a tortilla and keep the flavor, place the tortilla on a microwave-safe plate covered with a damp paper towel. Heat on HIGH for 30 seconds.

Honey Mustard-Glazed Ham

MAKES: 8 to 10 servings
HANDS-ON TIME: 6 min.
TOTAL TIME: 8 hours, 6 min.

1 (7- to 7¹/₂ -lb.) fully cooked, bone-in ham
³/₄ cup firmly packed light brown sugar
³/₄ cup honey
¹/₂ cup Dijon mustard
¹/₄ cup apple juice
Garnishes: orange wedges, red grapes, fresh parsley

❶ Remove skin and excess fat from ham. Score fat on ham, 1 inch apart, in a diamond pattern. Place ham in a 6-qt. oval slow cooker.

❷ Stir together brown sugar and next 3 ingredients in a small bowl. Brush brown sugar mixture over ham. Cover and cook on LOW 8 hours or until a meat thermometer registers 140°.

test kitchen note

We chose the shank portion of the ham because it fits in a slow cooker better and makes a prettier presentation than the butt portion. Examine the ham carefully before purchase to make sure that it isn't presliced.

Sausage, Red Beans, and Rice

MAKES: 8 servings
HANDS-ON TIME: 14 min.
TOTAL TIME: 16 hours, 14 min.

- 1 (16-oz.) package dried red beans
- 1 lb. smoked sausage, sliced
- 1 cup chopped onion
- $^{3}/_{4}$ cup chopped parsley
- 1 tsp. table salt
- $^{1}/_{2}$ tsp. dried oregano
- $^{1}/_{2}$ tsp. dried thyme
- Dash of ground red pepper
- 3 garlic cloves, minced
- Hot cooked rice
- Hot sauce
- Chopped green onions

1 Rinse and sort beans according to package directions. Cover with water 2 inches above beans; let soak 8 hours. Drain and place in a 5-qt. slow cooker.

2 Sauté sausage and onion in a large skillet over medium-high heat 5 minutes or until sausage is browned and onion is tender.

3 Stir sausage mixture, 5 cups water, parsley, and next 5 ingredients into beans. Cover and cook on LOW 8 hours. Mash beans with a potato masher or the back of a spoon to desired consistency. Serve with rice and hot sauce; sprinkle with green onions.

community chat

Easy, delicious, and healthy! You can also add a little more hot sauce if you like it spicy!

Spicy Asian Barbecued Drummettes

MAKES: 2 to 4 servings
HANDS-ON TIME: 8 min.
TOTAL TIME: 3 hours, 8 min.

3 lb. chicken drummettes (about 20)
1/2 tsp. table salt
1/4 tsp. black pepper
1 cup honey-barbecue sauce
1 Tbsp. Asian hot chili sauce (such as Sriracha)
1 Tbsp. soy sauce
3 garlic cloves, pressed
Garnishes: toasted sesame seeds, sliced green onions

1 Preheat broiler with oven rack 3 inches from heat.

2 Sprinkle drummettes with salt and pepper. Place on a lightly greased rack in a broiler pan. Broil 8 minutes or until browned. Place drummettes in a 4-qt. slow cooker.

3 Combine barbecue sauce and next 3 ingredients; pour over drummettes. Cover and cook on LOW 3 hours. Serve with sauce for dipping.

test kitchen note

Look for Sriracha hot chili sauce with the Asian foods on grocery shelves. It's a staple on the kitchen table in parts of Asia—much like ketchup is in the U.S. The blend of chiles, garlic, sugar, salt, and vinegar is very spicy.

Chicken Tetrazzini

MAKES: 8 to 10 servings
HANDS-ON TIME: 15 min.
TOTAL TIME: 4 hours, 25 min.

- 8 Tbsp. butter, divided
- 1 (8-oz.) package sliced fresh mushrooms
- 1 onion, chopped
- $1/2$ cup all-purpose flour
- 4 cups milk
- $1/4$ cup Marsala
- $1/2$ tsp. table salt
- $1/2$ tsp. freshly ground black pepper
- 12 oz. uncooked spaghetti, broken in half
- 4 cups chopped cooked chicken
- $1/2$ cup slivered almonds, toasted
- 2 cups freshly grated Parmigiano-Reggiano cheese

1 Melt 2 Tbsp. butter in a large deep skillet over medium-high heat. Add mushrooms and onion; sauté 3 to 4 minutes or until tender. Remove mushroom mixture, and set aside.

2 Melt remaining 6 Tbsp. butter in skillet; whisk in flour until smooth. Cook 1 minute, whisking constantly. Gradually whisk in milk; bring to a boil. Cook 2 to 3 minutes or until mixture thickens, stirring constantly. Stir in Marsala, salt, and black pepper.

3 Spoon one-third of milk mixture into a 5- or 6-qt. slow cooker. Top with half of spaghetti, half of mushroom mixture, half of chicken, half of almonds, and half of cheese. Repeat layers with one-third of milk mixture, and remaining spaghetti, mushroom mixture, chicken, and almonds. Top with remaining milk mixture; sprinkle with remaining cheese. Cover and cook on LOW 4 hours. Let stand 10 minutes before serving.

community chat

Chicken Tetrazzini is even better made in the slow cooker.

Featuring chicken, shrimp, and smoked sausage, this classic Creole rice dish is well-suited for the slow cooker because the slow cooking allows all the flavors to blend in a marvelous way.

Easy Jambalaya

MAKES: 8 servings

HANDS-ON TIME: 11 min.

TOTAL TIME: 5 hours, 41 min.

2 lb. skinned and boned chicken thighs

1 lb. smoked sausage, cut into 2-inch slices

1 (8-oz.) container refrigerated pre-chopped celery, onion, and bell pepper mix

1 (28-oz.) can diced tomatoes, undrained

3 garlic cloves, chopped

2 cups chicken broth

1 Tbsp. Cajun spice mix

1 tsp. dried thyme

1 tsp. dried oregano

$^3/_4$ lb. peeled, extra-large raw shrimp

$1^3/_4$ cups converted rice

Garnish: chopped parsley

1 Combine chicken, sausage, and next 7 ingredients in a 5-qt. slow cooker. Cover and cook on LOW 5 hours.

2 Add shrimp and rice, and increase heat to HIGH. Cover and cook 30 minutes.

community chat

This was absolutely delicious! You can add Old Bay seasoning in addition to the Cajun seasoning, and use a mixture of long grain rice and yellow saffron rice.

Smokehouse Chicken and Vegetable Stew

MAKES: 8 servings

HANDS-ON TIME: 5 min.

TOTAL TIME: 8 hours, 5 min.

Take pleasure in eating well without a lot of fuss. This vegetable-packed stew has a prep time of just 5 minutes.

1 cup chicken broth

$1/2$ cup sweet-and-spicy barbecue sauce

$1^{1}/_{4}$ cups refrigerated prechopped tri-color bell pepper

1 cup frozen baby lima beans

2 Tbsp. Worcestershire sauce

$1/2$ tsp. table salt

$1/2$ tsp. black pepper

2 lb. pulled smoked chicken

1 (26-oz.) jar fire-roasted tomato and garlic pasta sauce

1 (16-oz.) package frozen mixed vegetables

1 (8-oz.) container refrigerated prechopped onion

Combine all ingredients in a 5-qt. slow cooker. Cover and cook on HIGH 8 hours.

test kitchen note

A snug-fitting, see-through lid works best. Removing the lid during cooking releases a great deal of heat, so you want to be able to see your food through the lid rather than having to lift it.

Chicken Marsala

MAKES: 8 servings
HANDS-ON TIME: 20 min.
TOTAL TIME: 6 hours, 30 min.

2 cloves garlic, finely chopped
1 Tbsp. vegetable oil
8 skinned and boned chicken breasts
$\frac{1}{2}$ tsp. table salt
$\frac{1}{2}$ tsp. black pepper
2 (6-oz.) jars sliced mushrooms, drained
1 cup sweet Marsala wine or chicken broth
$\frac{1}{4}$ cup cornstarch
Hot cooked rice
Garnish: chopped fresh parsley

❶ Mix garlic and oil in a lightly greased 4- or 5-qt. slow cooker. Sprinkle chicken with salt and black pepper; place over garlic. Place mushrooms over chicken; pour wine over all.

❷ Cover and cook on LOW 5 to 6 hours.

❸ Remove chicken from slow cooker; cover to keep warm. In small bowl, mix $\frac{1}{2}$ cup water and cornstarch until smooth; stir into liquid in slow cooker. Increase heat to HIGH. Cover and cook about 10 minutes or until sauce is slightly thickened.

❹ Return chicken to slow cooker. Cover and cook on HIGH 5 minutes or until hot. Serve over rice.

community chat

This is a great dish to make for company—especially during a busy week.

Chicken Parmesan

MAKES: 6 servings
HANDS-ON TIME: 12 min.
TOTAL TIME: 3 hours, 47 min.

2 cups Italian-seasoned panko (Japanese breadcrumbs)
6 skinned and boned chicken breasts
2 large eggs, lightly beaten
4 Tbsp. olive oil
1 (44-oz.) jar tomato-basil pasta sauce
$^3/_4$ tsp. table salt
$^1/_2$ tsp. black pepper
1 (8-oz.) package shredded mozzarella cheese
$^3/_4$ cup (3 oz.) shredded Parmesan cheese
Cooked spaghetti
Garnish: fresh oregano

1 Spread breadcrumbs on a large plate. Dip chicken in beaten egg, 1 breast at a time. Dredge chicken in bread-crumbs, pressing crumbs gently to adhere.

2 Heat 2 Tbsp. oil in a large nonstick skillet over medium-high heat. Cook chicken, in 2 batches, 2 minutes on each side or until browned, adding remaining 2 Tbsp. oil with second batch.

3 Pour pasta sauce into a lightly greased 6- or 7-qt. oval slow cooker. Arrange chicken in slow cooker over sauce. Sprinkle with salt and black pepper. Cover and cook on HIGH 3½ hours. Add cheeses; cover and cook on HIGH 5 more minutes or until cheese melts. Serve over spaghetti.

community chat

This dinner is great for kids. And best of all, cleanup is a breeze!

Turkey Meatball Stroganoff

MAKES: 6 servings

HANDS-ON TIME: 20 min.

TOTAL TIME: 7 hours, 35 min.

1 lb. lean ground turkey
$^1/_2$ cup soft breadcrumbs
$^1/_2$ cup finely chopped onion
1 tsp. country-style Dijon mustard
$^1/_2$ tsp. table salt
$^1/_2$ tsp. freshly ground black pepper
2 (8-oz.) packages fresh mushrooms, quartered
1 (14-oz.) can reduced-sodium beef broth
5 cups uncooked wide egg noodles
$^1/_3$ cup all-purpose flour
$^1/_3$ cup cold water
1 (12-oz.) container light French onion dip
Garnish: chopped fresh parsley

❶ In medium bowl, mix turkey, breadcrumbs, onion, mustard, salt, and black pepper. Shape mixture into 16 meatballs, and add to a lightly greased medium nonstick skillet. Cook over medium-high heat until brown. Place meatballs in a lightly greased $3^1/_2$- or 4-qt. oval slow cooker; top with mushrooms. Add broth.

❷ Cover and cook on LOW 6 to 7 hours.

❸ Prepare noodles according to package directions. Remove meatballs and mushrooms from slow cooker using slotted spoon; cover to keep warm. In small bowl, mix flour and water; gradually stir into slow cooker until blended. Increase heat to HIGH. Cover and cook on HIGH 15 to 20 minutes or until thickened. Stir in dip; heat until hot. Stir in meatballs and mushrooms. Serve over noodles.

shortcut secret

Meatballs freeze well so you can make them ahead and freeze until ready to eat.

Orange-Rosemary Poached Salmon

MAKES: 4 servings
HANDS-ON TIME: 9 min.
TOTAL TIME: 2 hours, 39 min.

test kitchen note

Select fillets from the ends of the salmon. These are thinner than those cut from the center of the fish.

1 cup orange juice
1 cup vegetable broth
$^1/_2$ cup fresh parsley leaves
3 Tbsp. butter
6 garlic cloves, pressed
2 (5-inch) sprigs fresh rosemary
1 navel orange, sliced
4 (6-oz.) skinless salmon fillets ($^1/_2$ to $^3/_4$ inch thick)

1 tsp. salt
2 tsp. orange zest
$^1/_2$ tsp. freshly ground black pepper
$^1/_4$ tsp. ground red pepper
Hot cooked orzo
Sautéed baby bok choy

❶ Place first 7 ingredients in a 5-qt. oval slow cooker. Cover and cook on HIGH 2 hours.

❷ Meanwhile, sprinkle salmon with salt, orange zest, and peppers. Cover and chill 2 hours.

❸ Place salmon in liquid in slow cooker. Cover and cook 30 more minutes or until desired degree of doneness. Carefully transfer salmon to a serving platter using a large spatula. Serve over hot cooked orzo and sautéed baby bok choy.

Greek Snapper

MAKES: 4 servings

HANDS-ON TIME: 9 min.

TOTAL TIME: 3 hours, 9 min.

1½ cups dry white wine
1 cup thinly sliced onion
3 garlic cloves, minced
2 bay leaves
4 (6-oz.) red snapper fillets (1 inch thick)
4 plum tomatoes, chopped
1 tsp. dried oregano
½ tsp. table salt
½ tsp. freshly ground black pepper
1 Tbsp. olive oil
Hot cooked rice
1 oz. crumbled feta cheese
Lemon wedges
Garnish: fresh oregano

❶ Combine first 4 ingredients in a 6-qt. oval slow cooker. Cover and cook on HIGH 1 hour.

❷ Add fish to slow cooker in a single layer. Combine tomato and next 3 ingredients in a bowl; spoon over fish. Drizzle oil over fish. Reduce heat to LOW; cover and cook 2 hours.

❸ Carefully remove fish from cooking liquid. Serve over rice. Spoon tomato mixture over fish. Sprinkle with feta cheese, and serve with lemon wedges.

make it a meal

Serve this with steamed asparagus for a quick and healthy dinner.

1 Tbsp. canola oil
$^1/_2$ cup refrigerated prechopped onion
1 (12-oz.) package frozen meatless burger crumbles
$^1/_2$ tsp. chili powder
$^1/_2$ tsp. ground cumin
2 (11-oz.) cans yellow corn with red and green bell peppers, drained
Heavy-duty aluminum foil
1 (16-oz.) can refried beans
6 (6-inch) fajita-size flour tortillas
$1^2/_3$ cups fresh salsa
$2^3/_4$ cups (11 oz.) shredded Monterey Jack cheese
Toppings: sour cream, chopped fresh cilantro, shredded Monterey Jack cheese, fresh salsa, guacamole

Layered Mexican Tortilla Pie

MAKES: 6 to 8 servings
HANDS-ON TIME: 15 min.
TOTAL TIME: 3 hours, 15 min.

1 Heat oil in a large nonstick skillet over medium-high heat. Add onion; cook 3 minutes or until tender. Stir in burger crumbles and next 3 ingredients. Cook 2 minutes or until crumbles are thawed. Remove from heat.

2 Fold 2 (17- x 12-inch) sheets of heavy-duty aluminum foil into 2 (17- x 2-inch) strips. Arrange strips in an "X" pattern in a lightly greased 4-qt. round slow cooker, allowing foil to extend 1 inch beyond edges of slow cooker.

3 Spread about $^1/_3$ cup refried beans on each of 5 tortillas. Place 1 tortilla, bean side up, on top of foil X in slow cooker. Spoon 1 cup burger mixture over beans; top with $^1/_3$ cup salsa and $^1/_2$ cup cheese. Repeat layers 4 times. Top with remaining tortilla, and sprinkle with remaining $^1/_4$ cup cheese. Cover and cook on LOW 3 hours or until cheese melts and edges are bubbly.

4 Remove insert from slow cooker; let stand, uncovered, 15 minutes. Grasping ends of foil strips, carefully transfer pie to a serving plate. Carefully remove foil strips. Cut pie into wedges, and serve with desired toppings.

shortcut secret

Purchase cheese in bulk and shred it ahead of time. Store in the freezer to have on hand as needed.

Loaded Potato Soup

MAKES: 8 servings

HANDS-ON TIME: 15 min.

TOTAL TIME: 8 hours, 35 min.

4 lb. new potatoes, peeled and cut into $1/4$-inch-thick slices
1 small onion, chopped
2 (14-oz.) cans chicken broth
2 tsp. table salt
$1/2$ tsp. black pepper
2 cups half-and-half
Toppings: shredded Cheddar cheese, cooked and crumbled bacon, sliced green onions

❶ Layer sliced potatoes in a lightly greased 5-qt. slow cooker; top with chopped onion.

❷ Stir together broth, salt, and black pepper; pour over potatoes and onion. (Broth will not completely cover potatoes and onion.) Cover and cook on LOW 8 hours or until potatoes are tender. Mash mixture with a potato masher; stir in half-and-half. Cover and cook on HIGH 20 more minutes or until mixture is thoroughly heated. Ladle into bowls, and serve with desired toppings.

make it a meal

Serve this scrumptious soup with a big tossed salad and some of your favorite bakery bread.

7

Anytime Breakfast Favorites

*Enjoy some morning favorites
for a quick evening supper.*

Peanut oil
2 cups sliced fresh okra
$^1/_2$ green bell pepper, diced
$^1/_2$ medium onion, diced
1 large egg
$^1/_2$ cup all-purpose flour
$^1/_4$ cup heavy cream
1 jalapeño pepper, finely chopped
$^3/_4$ tsp. table salt
$^1/_4$ tsp. freshly ground black pepper
$^1/_4$ lb. unpeeled, medium-size raw shrimp, peeled and coarsely chopped
Fresh Tomato Salsa
Cilantro Sour Cream

1 Pour oil to depth of 3 inches in a Dutch oven; heat to 350°.

2 Stir together okra and next 8 ingredients in a large bowl until well blended; stir in shrimp.

3 Drop batter by rounded tablespoonfuls into hot oil, and fry, in batches, 2 to 3 minutes on each side or until golden brown. Drain on a wire rack over paper towels. Serve with Fresh Tomato Salsa and Cilantro Sour Cream.

Fresh Tomato Salsa

Stir together 4 large plum tomatoes, seeded and chopped (about 2 cups); $^1/_4$ cup chopped fresh cilantro; 1 jalapeño pepper, seeded and finely diced; 3 Tbsp. finely diced red onion; $2^1/_2$ Tbsp. fresh lime juice; 1 Tbsp. extra virgin olive oil; and salt and pepper to taste. **MAKES:** 4 servings; **HANDS-ON TIME:** 15 min.; **TOTAL TIME:** 15 min.

Cilantro Sour Cream

Stir together 1 (8-oz.) container sour cream, $^1/_4$ cup chopped fresh cilantro, 1 tsp. lime zest, 1 tsp. fresh lime juice, and salt and pepper to taste. **MAKES:** 1 cup; **HANDS-ON TIME:** 5 min.; **TOTAL TIME:** 5 min.

TOP **5** BREAKFAST RECIPES

Okra-Shrimp Beignets

MAKES: about 30 beignets

HANDS-ON TIME: 27 min.

TOTAL TIME: 47 min., including salsa and sour cream

test kitchen note

We took two Lowcountry favorites, okra and shrimp, and fried them into fritters that have the crispy and airy qualities of a good beignet, hence the name.

TOP 5 BREAKFAST RECIPES

English Muffin French Toast

MAKES: 6 servings
HANDS-ON TIME: 20 min.
TOTAL TIME: 8 hours, 20 min.

This lightened version of French toast is made with English muffins instead of French bread, nonfat buttermilk instead of whole milk, and features Greek yogurt and fresh fruit.

4 large eggs
1 cup nonfat buttermilk
2 tsp. orange zest
1 tsp. vanilla extract
6 English muffins, split
Vegetable cooking spray
1 cup fat-free Greek yogurt
2 Tbsp. maple syrup
Toppings: chopped fresh strawberries, chopped fresh nectarines

❶ Whisk together first 4 ingredients in a bowl. Place English muffins in a 13- x 9-inch baking dish, overlapping edges. Pour egg mixture over muffins. Cover and chill 8 to 12 hours.

❷ Remove muffins from remaining liquid, discarding liquid.

❸ Cook muffins, in batches, in a large skillet coated with cooking spray over medium-high heat 2 to 3 minutes on each side or until muffins are golden. Stir together yogurt and syrup until blended; serve with muffin French toast and toppings.

community chat

This dish is easy and delicious—perfect for a light spring or summer supper.

4 frozen biscuits
2 Tbsp. butter, melted
3 Tbsp. chopped fresh chives, divided
1 (0.9-oz.) envelope hollandaise sauce mix
1 cup milk
1 Tbsp. lemon juice

$^3/_4$ cup chopped lean ham
$^1/_4$ to $^1/_2$ tsp. ground red pepper
$^1/_2$ tsp. white vinegar
4 large eggs
2 cups loosely packed arugula
1 small avocado, sliced

Spicy Ham-And-Eggs Benedict
with Chive Biscuits

MAKES: 4 servings
HANDS-ON TIME: 30 min.
TOTAL TIME: 55 min.

1 Bake biscuits according to package directions. Combine melted butter and 1 Tbsp. chives; split biscuits, and brush with butter mixture. Preheat oven to 375°. Place biscuits, buttered sides up, on a baking sheet, and bake at 375° for 5 minutes or until toasted.

2 Prepare hollandaise sauce mix according to package directions, using milk and lemon juice and omitting butter.

3 Cook ham, stirring occasionally, in a medium-size nonstick skillet over medium heat 3 to 4 minutes or until browned. Stir ham and red pepper into hollandaise sauce; keep warm.

4 Add water to depth of 2 inches in a large saucepan. Bring to a boil; reduce heat, and maintain at a light simmer. Add white vinegar. Break eggs, and slip into water, 1 at a time, as close as possible to surface of water. Simmer 3 to 5 minutes or to desired degree of doneness. Remove with a slotted spoon. Trim edges, if desired.

5 Place bottom biscuit halves, buttered sides up, on each of 4 individual serving plates. Top with arugula, avocado, and poached eggs. Spoon hollandaise sauce evenly on top of each egg. Sprinkle with remaining 2 Tbsp. chives and pepper to taste. Top with remaining biscuit halves, and serve immediately.

NOTE: We tested with White Lily Southern Style Biscuits.

community chat

This dish was delicious—everyone loved it. Serve it with a cheesy potato casserole.

TOP **5** BREAKFAST RECIPES

SAUSAGE-AND-EGG CASSEROLE-

MAKES: 10 servings
HANDS-ON TIME: 20 min.
TOTAL TIME: 45 min.

shortcut secret

Freeze the casserole ahead to have it for a quick meal. Wrap unbaked casserole with plastic wrap, then foil, and label and freeze up to 1 month. To reheat, thaw in the fridge overnight. Bake as directed in Step 3.

8 ($1^1/_2$-oz.) sourdough bread slices, cut into $^1/_2$-inch cubes
1 (12-oz.) package fully cooked pork sausage patties, chopped
$2^1/_2$ cups 2% reduced-fat milk

4 large eggs
1 Tbsp. Dijon mustard
$^1/_2$ cup buttermilk
1 ($10^3/_4$-oz.) can cream of mushroom soup
1 cup (4 oz.) shredded sharp Cheddar cheese

❶ Preheat oven to 350°. Arrange bread in 2 lightly greased 8-inch square baking dishes or 1 lightly greased 13- x 9-inch baking dish. Top evenly with sausage. Whisk together milk, eggs, and Dijon mustard. Pour evenly over bread mixture.

❷ Whisk together buttermilk and cream of mushroom soup. Spoon over bread mixture; sprinkle with Cheddar cheese. Place casserole on a baking sheet.

❸ Bake at 350° for 1 hour or until casserole is set. Serve immediately.

4 (1/2-inch-thick) challah bread slices
2 Tbsp. butter, melted
1 (0.9-oz.) envelope hollandaise sauce mix
1/4 tsp. lemon zest
1 1/2 tsp. fresh lemon juice, divided
2 cups loosely packed arugula
1/2 cup loosely packed fresh flat-leaf parsley leaves
1/4 cup thinly sliced red onion
3 tsp. extra virgin olive oil
4 large eggs
1/4 tsp. kosher salt
1/4 tsp. freshly ground black pepper
12 thin pancetta slices, cooked
2 Tbsp. chopped sun-dried tomatoes

Fried Egg Sandwiches

MAKES: 4 servings

HANDS-ON TIME: 25 min.

TOTAL TIME: 27 min.

❶ Preheat broiler with oven rack 5 to 6 inches from heat. Brush both sides of bread with butter; place on an aluminum foil-lined broiler pan. Broil 1 to 2 minutes on each side or until lightly toasted. Prepare hollandaise sauce according to package directions; stir in zest and 1/2 tsp. lemon juice. Keep warm.

❷ Toss together arugula, next 2 ingredients, 2 tsp. oil, and remaining 1 tsp. lemon juice. Heat remaining 1 tsp. olive oil in a large nonstick skillet over medium heat. Gently break eggs into hot skillet; sprinkle with salt and pepper. Cook 2 to 3 minutes on each side or to desired degree of doneness.

❸ Top bread slices with arugula mixture, pancetta slices, and fried eggs. Spoon hollandaise sauce over each egg, and sprinkle with tomatoes. Serve immediately.

make it a meal

Serve this one-dish meal with a side of fresh fruit for a well-balanced supper.

12 large eggs
1 cup half-and-half
1/2 tsp. table salt
1/4 tsp. freshly ground black pepper
2 Tbsp. chopped fresh chives
1 Tbsp. chopped fresh parsley
1 tsp. chopped fresh oregano
1 pt. grape tomatoes, halved
1 1/2 cups (6 oz.) shredded Italian three-cheese blend

Tomato-Herb Mini Frittatas

MAKES: 8 servings
HANDS-ON TIME: 15 min.
TOTAL TIME: 30 min.

❶ Preheat oven to 450°. Process eggs and next 3 ingredients in a blender until blended. Stir together chives and next 2 ingredients in a small bowl. Place 8 lightly greased 4-inch (6-oz.) ramekins on 2 baking sheets; layer tomatoes, 1 cup cheese, and chive mixture in ramekins. Pour egg mixture over top, and sprinkle with remaining 1/2 cup cheese.

❷ Bake at 450° for 7 minutes, placing 1 baking sheet on middle oven rack and other on lower oven rack. Switch baking sheets, and bake 7 to 8 more minutes or until set. Remove top baking sheet from oven; transfer bottom sheet to middle rack, and bake 1 to 2 more minutes or until lightly browned.

test kitchen note

Transferring the bottom baking sheet to the middle rack during the last few minutes of cooking time allows the top to brown slightly.

Grits-and-Greens Breakfast Bake

MAKES: 8 servings
HANDS-ON TIME: 25 min.
TOTAL TIME: 2 hours, 7 min.

1 tsp. table salt
1½ cups uncooked quick-cooking grits
1 cup (4 oz.) shredded white Cheddar cheese
3 Tbsp. butter
½ cup half-and-half
¼ tsp. freshly ground black pepper
¼ tsp. ground red pepper
2 large eggs
3 cups Simple Collard Greens, drained
8 large eggs
Hot sauce (optional)

❶ Preheat oven to 375°. Bring salt and 4 cups water to a boil in a large saucepan over medium-high heat; gradually whisk in grits. Reduce heat to medium, and cook, whisking often, 5 to 7 minutes or until thickened. Remove from heat, and stir in cheese and butter.

❷ Whisk together half-and-half, next 2 ingredients, and 2 eggs in a medium bowl. Stir half-and-half mixture into grits mixture. Stir in Simple Collard Greens. Pour mixture into a lightly greased 13- x 9-inch baking dish.

❸ Bake at 375° for 25 to 30 minutes or until set. Remove from oven.

❹ Make 8 indentations in grits mixture with back of a large spoon. Break remaining 8 eggs, 1 at a time, and slip 1 egg into each indentation. Bake at 375° for 12 to 14 minutes or until eggs are cooked to desired degree of doneness. Cover loosely with aluminum foil, and let stand 10 minutes. Serve with hot sauce, if desired.

Simple Collard Greens:

Cook ½ medium-size chopped onion in 2 Tbsp. hot oil in a large Dutch oven over medium heat, stirring occasionally, 10 minutes or until tender. Add 1 (16-oz.) package washed, trimmed, and chopped collard greens; 1½ tsp. salt; and 3 cups water. Bring to a boil; reduce heat, and simmer 30 minutes or until tender. MAKES: 3 cups; HANDS-ON TIME: 10 min.; TOTAL TIME: 50 min.

shortcut secret

Give yourself a head start: Make Simple Collard Greens up to three days ahead.

Sunny Skillet Breakfast

MAKES: 6 servings
HANDS-ON TIME: 31 min.
TOTAL TIME: 51 min.

Great recipe! You can easily add your favorite veggies or change up the cheese. This will also be a perfect meal when camping for breakfast or dinner.

3 (8-oz.) baking potatoes, peeled and shredded (about 3 cups firmly packed)*
1 Tbsp. butter
2 Tbsp. vegetable oil
1 small red bell pepper, diced
1 medium onion, diced
1 garlic clove, pressed
3/4 tsp. table salt, divided
6 large eggs
1/4 tsp. black pepper

❶ Preheat oven to 350°. Place shredded potatoes in a large bowl; add cold water to cover. Let stand 5 minutes; drain and pat dry.

❷ Melt butter with oil in a 10-inch cast-iron skillet over medium heat. Add bell pepper and onion, and sauté 3 to 5 minutes or until tender. Add garlic; sauté 1 minute. Stir in shredded potatoes and 1/2 tsp. salt; cook, stirring often, 10 minutes or until potatoes are golden and tender.

❸ Remove from heat. Make 6 indentations in potato mixture, using back of a spoon. Break 1 egg into each indentation. Sprinkle eggs with pepper and remaining 1/4 tsp. salt.

❹ Bake at 350° for 12 to 14 minutes or until eggs are set. Serve immediately.

* 3 cups firmly packed frozen shredded potatoes may be substituted, omitting Step 1.

<table>
<tr><td>2 large eggs</td><td>¹/₈ tsp. table salt</td></tr>
</table>

2 large eggs
1 Tbsp. butter
1 cup coarsely chopped
   spinach
$^1/_3$ cup chopped tomatoes

$^1/_8$ tsp. table salt
$^1/_3$ cup (1$^1/_2$ oz.)
   shredded Swiss
   cheese
$^1/_8$ tsp. black pepper

1 Process eggs and 2 Tbsp. water in a blender until blended. Melt butter in an 8-inch nonstick skillet over medium heat; add spinach and tomatoes, and sauté 1 minute or until spinach is wilted. Add salt and egg mixture to skillet.

2 As egg mixture starts to cook, gently lift edges of omelet with a spatula, and tilt pan so uncooked egg mixture flows underneath, cooking until almost set (about 1 minute). Cover skillet, and cook 1 minute.

3 Sprinkle omelet with cheese and pepper. Fold omelet in half, allowing cheese to melt. Slide cooked omelet onto a serving plate. Add salt to taste.

Spinach-and-Cheese Omelet

MAKES: 1 serving
HANDS-ON TIME: 14 min.
TOTAL TIME: 14 min.

test kitchen note

Add extra nutrients to your meal by stirring chopped fresh spinach, chopped tomato, and shredded cheese into your protein-packed omelet.

8 (4-oz.) chicken breast cutlets, cut in half crosswise
2 cups dill pickle juice from jar
2 large eggs
3/4 cup self-rising cornmeal mix

3/4 cup fine, dry breadcrumbs
1/4 cup finely chopped fresh parsley
1 tsp. black pepper
1/2 tsp. table salt
1 cup peanut oil
Cornbread Biscuits

Crispy Chicken Cutlets

MAKES: 16 servings

HANDS-ON TIME: 30 min.

TOTAL TIME: 8 hours, 30 min.

❶ Combine first 2 ingredients in a large zip-top plastic freezer bag. Seal bag, pressing out most of air, and chill 8 hours.

❷ Whisk together eggs and 3 Tbsp. water in a shallow bowl. Combine cornmeal mix and next 3 ingredients in a second shallow bowl. Remove chicken from marinade, discarding marinade; sprinkle chicken with salt. Dip chicken in egg mixture, and dredge in cornmeal mixture, pressing firmly to adhere.

❸ Heat oil in a large nonstick skillet over medium-high heat. Add chicken, and cook, in batches, 2 to 3 minutes on each side or until done. Serve in Cornbread Biscuits.

Cornbread Biscuits:

❶ Preheat oven to 500°. Whisk together 3 cups self-rising soft-wheat flour and 1/2 cup yellow self-rising cornmeal mix in a large bowl. Cut in 1/4 cup cold butter, cut into pieces, and 1/4 cup shortening with a pastry blender until mixture resembles small peas and dough is crumbly. Cover and chill 10 minutes. Add 1 1/2 cups buttermilk, stirring just until dry ingredients are moistened.

❷ Turn dough out onto a heavily floured surface; knead 3 or 4 times. Pat dough into a 3/4-inch-thick circle. Cut dough with a well-floured 2 1/2-inch round cutter, rerolling scraps as needed. Sprinkle 1 tsp. cornmeal on ungreased baking sheets; place biscuits on baking sheets. Lightly brush tops with 2 Tbsp. melted butter. Bake at 500° for 13 to 15 minutes or until golden brown. **MAKES:** about 15 biscuits; **HANDS-ON TIME:** 30 min.; **TOTAL TIME:** 53 min.

test kitchen note

These taste similar to the chicken from a certain closed-on-Sunday fast-food chain that folks love. The secret? Dill pickle juice!

Sweet Peach Pancakes

MAKES: 10 pancakes
HANDS-ON TIME: 1 hour, 5 min.
TOTAL TIME: 1 hour, 5 min.

The sweetness of the peaches combined with the natural sweetness of the cornmeal makes for a delicious morning.

$3/4$ cup all-purpose soft-wheat flour
$3/4$ cup plain yellow cornmeal
2 Tbsp. sugar
$1/2$ tsp. baking powder
$1/2$ tsp. baking soda
$1/2$ tsp. table salt
$1^{1}/4$ cups buttermilk
2 large eggs
2 Tbsp. unsalted butter, melted

Butter
Canola oil
3 medium peaches (about $1^{1}/4$ lb.), unpeeled and cut into 10 thin wedges each*
Garnishes: sweetened whipped cream, syrup, fresh mint

1 Sift together first 6 ingredients in a large bowl. Whisk together buttermilk, eggs, and melted butter in a medium bowl. Add buttermilk mixture to flour mixture, and whisk just until combined.

2 Melt a small amount of butter with oil on a griddle or large nonstick skillet over medium heat. Place 3 peach wedges for each pancake on griddle; starting at outside edge of peach slices, carefully pour $1/4$ cup batter over each group of slices to form a circle.

3 Cook pancakes 3 to 4 minutes or until tops are covered with bubbles and edges look dry and cooked. Turn and cook other sides 2 to 3 minutes or until golden. Transfer to a baking sheet; keep warm in a 300° oven. Repeat procedure with remaining peach slices and batter, adding more butter and oil to griddle as needed.

NOTE: We tested with White Lily All-Purpose Soft Wheat Flour.

* 2 medium peaches, unpeeled and diced, may be substituted. Stir into batter at end of Step 1. Cook pancakes as directed, using $1/4$ cup batter per pancake.

community chat

A well-seasoned griddle or skillet won't need as much butter and oil; use only as much as you need to keep the pancakes from sticking.

1$\frac{3}{4}$ cups all-purpose flour
2 tsp. sugar
1$\frac{1}{2}$ tsp. baking powder
1 tsp. baking soda
1 tsp. table salt
2 cups buttermilk
2 large eggs
$\frac{1}{4}$ cup butter, melted
Buttered Honey Syrup

1 Combine flour and next 4 ingredients in a large bowl. Whisk together buttermilk and eggs. Gradually stir buttermilk mixture into flour mixture. Gently stir in butter. (Batter will be lumpy.)

2 Pour about $\frac{1}{4}$ cup batter for each pancake onto a hot buttered griddle or large nonstick skillet. Cook pancakes 3 to 4 minutes or until tops are covered with bubbles and edges look dry and cooked. Turn and cook 3 to 4 minutes or until golden brown. Place pancakes in a single layer on a baking sheet, and keep warm in a 200° oven up to 30 minutes. Serve with Buttered Honey Syrup.

Buttered Honey Syrup:

Melt $\frac{1}{3}$ cup butter in a small saucepan over medium-low heat. Stir in $\frac{1}{2}$ cup honey, and cook 1 minute or until warm. **MAKES:** $\frac{3}{4}$ cup; **HANDS-ON TIME:** 5 min.; **TOTAL TIME:** 34 min.

NOTE: Buttered Honey Syrup cannot be made ahead. The heated honey will crystallize when cooled and will not melt if reheated.

Pam Cakes
With Buttered Honey Syrup

MAKES: 16 (4-inch) pancakes
HANDS-ON TIME: 34 min.
TOTAL TIME: 34 min.

test kitchen note

Use a light hand when stirring the batter; overmixing will cause a rubbery texture. When using a griddle to cook pancakes, set the temperature dial to 350°.

One-Dish Blackberry French Toast

MAKES: 8 to 10 servings
HANDS-ON TIME: 21 min.
TOTAL TIME: 8 hours, 51 min.

This French toast recipe is loaded with tasty, sweet ingredients, but you can always add a little extra sweetness with maple syrup or whipped cream.

1 cup blackberry jam
1 (12-oz.) French bread loaf, cut into 1½-inch cubes
1 (8-oz.) package ⅓-less-fat cream cheese, cut into 1-inch cubes
4 large eggs
2 cups half-and-half
1 tsp. ground cinnamon
1 tsp. vanilla extract
½ cup firmly packed brown sugar
Toppings: maple syrup, whipped cream

❶ Cook jam in a small saucepan over medium heat 1 to 2 minutes or until melted and smooth, stirring once.

❷ Place half of bread cubes in bottom of a lightly greased 13- x 9-inch baking dish. Top with cream cheese cubes, and drizzle with melted jam. Top with remaining bread cubes.

❸ Whisk together eggs and next 3 ingredients. Pour over bread mixture. Sprinkle with brown sugar. Cover tightly, and chill 8 to 24 hours.

❹ Preheat oven to 325°. Bake, covered, 20 minutes. Uncover and bake 10 to 15 minutes or until bread is golden brown and mixture is set. Serve with desired toppings.

community chat

Super easy! Very tasty! Serve this with fresh blackberries and syrup.

8

Pizza & Pasta Dishes

Skip delivery, and serve your family these fresh favorites in a hurry.

TOP **5** PIZZAS & PASTAS

Tomato-and-Corn Pizza

MAKES: 4 servings
HANDS-ON TIME: 10 min.
TOTAL TIME: 44 min.

3 small plum tomatoes, sliced
$1/4$ tsp. table salt
Dash of freshly ground black pepper
1 (14-oz.) package prebaked Italian pizza crust
Parchment paper
$1/3$ cup refrigerated pesto
$1/2$ cup fresh corn kernels
$1/4$ cup grated Parmesan cheese
1 tsp. sugar
8 oz. fresh mozzarella, sliced
3 Tbsp. fresh whole or torn basil leaves

❶ Preheat oven to 450°. Place tomato slices on paper towels. Sprinkle with salt and pepper; let stand 20 minutes.

❷ Place pizza crust on a parchment paper-lined baking sheet; spread with pesto. Stir together corn, Parmesan, and sugar. Top pizza with corn mixture, tomatoes, and mozzarella slices.

❸ Bake at 450° for 14 minutes or until crust is golden and cheese is melted. Remove from oven, and top with basil leaves.

NOTE: We tested with Boboli Original Pizza Crust.

community chat

This pizza is a great summer evening meal. It's perfect with corn from the farmers' market and tomatoes and basil from the garden. A delicious, healthy meal.

Vegetable cooking spray
1 lb. unpeeled, large raw shrimp
1 large yellow onion, chopped
1 red bell pepper, chopped
1/4 tsp. table salt
1/4 tsp. black pepper
1 1/2 tsp. olive oil
1 1/2 lb. bakery pizza dough
All-purpose flour
Plain yellow cornmeal
1/2 cup commercial pesto
3/4 cup freshly grated Parmesan cheese

TOP 5 PIZZAS & PASTAS

Shrimp-Pesto Pizza

MAKES: 6 servings
HANDS-ON TIME: 20 min.
TOTAL TIME: 40 min.

1 Coat cold cooking grate of grill with cooking spray, and place on grill. Preheat grill to 350° (medium) heat. Peel shrimp, and slice in half lengthwise; devein, if desired.

2 Sauté onion, bell pepper, salt, and pepper in 1/2 tsp. hot oil in a large skillet over medium heat 5 minutes or until tender. Transfer onion mixture to a large bowl. Sauté shrimp in remaining 1 tsp. hot oil 3 minutes or just until shrimp turn pink. Add shrimp to onion mixture, and toss.

3 Divide dough into 6 equal portions. Lightly sprinkle flour on a large surface. Roll each portion into a 6-inch round (about 1/4-inch thick). Carefully transfer pizza dough rounds to a cutting board or baking sheet sprinkled with cornmeal.

4 Slide pizza dough rounds onto cooking grate of grill; spread pesto over rounds, and top with shrimp mixture. Sprinkle each with 2 Tbsp. Parmesan cheese. Grill, covered with grill lid, 4 minutes. Rotate pizzas one-quarter turn, and grill, covered with grill lid, 5 to 6 more minutes or until pizza crusts are golden. Serve immediately.

test kitchen note

We found fresh pizza dough available behind the deli counter at Publix. If you're expecting a larger crowd, you can buy pizza dough in bulk from your local wholesale club or even a favorite pizza restaurant.

TOP **5** PIZZAS & PASTAS

Grilled Tomato-Peach Pizza

MAKES: 4 servings
HANDS-ON TIME: 26 min.
TOTAL TIME: 26 min.

make it a meal

Perfect for a spring or summer cookout, serve this one-dish meal on its own or with mixed salad greens. End your meal with ice cream sundaes.

Vegetable cooking spray
2 tomatoes, sliced
$^1/_2$ tsp. table salt
1 large peach, peeled and sliced
1 lb. bakery pizza dough
$^1/_2$ (16-oz.) package fresh mozzarella, sliced
4 to 6 fresh basil leaves
Garnishes: coarsely ground pepper, olive oil

1 Coat cold cooking grate of grill with cooking spray, and place on grill. Preheat grill to 350° (medium) heat.

2 Sprinkle tomatoes with salt; let stand 15 minutes. Pat tomatoes dry with paper towels.

3 Grill peach slices, covered with grill lid, 2 to 3 minutes on each side or until grill marks appear.

4 Place dough on a large baking sheet coated with cooking spray; lightly coat dough with cooking spray. Roll dough to $^1/_4$-inch thickness (about 14 inches in diameter). Slide pizza dough from baking sheet onto cooking grate.

5 Grill, covered with grill lid, 2 to 3 minutes or until lightly browned. Turn dough over, and reduce temperature to 250° to 300° (low) heat; top with tomatoes, grilled peaches, and mozzarella. Grill, covered with grill lid, 5 minutes or until crust is golden and cheese is melted. Arrange basil leaves over pizza. Serve immediately.

- 1 (12-oz.) package farfalle (bow-tie) pasta
- 5 Tbsp. butter, divided
- 1 medium onion, chopped
- 1 medium-size red bell pepper, chopped
- 1 (8-oz.) package fresh mushrooms, quartered
- 1/3 cup all-purpose flour
- 3 cups chicken broth
- 2 cups milk
- 3 cups chopped cooked chicken
- 1 cup (4 oz.) shredded Parmesan cheese
- 1 tsp. black pepper
- 1/2 tsp. table salt
- Toppings: toasted sliced almonds, chopped fresh flat-leaf parsley, shredded Parmesan cheese

One-Dish Chicken Pasta

MAKES: 6 servings
HANDS-ON TIME: 30 min.
TOTAL TIME: 30 min.

1 Prepare pasta according to package directions. Meanwhile, melt 2 Tbsp. butter in a Dutch oven over medium heat. Add onion and bell pepper; sauté 5 minutes or until tender. Add mushrooms; sauté 4 minutes. Remove from Dutch oven.

2 Melt remaining 3 Tbsp. butter in Dutch oven over low heat; whisk in flour until smooth. Cook, whisking constantly, 1 minute. Gradually whisk in chicken broth and milk; cook over medium heat, whisking constantly, 5 to 7 minutes or until thickened and bubbly.

3 Stir chicken, sautéed vegetables, and hot cooked pasta into sauce. Add cheese, pepper, and salt. Serve with desired toppings.

test kitchen note

Partially freeze meat and chicken so it's quick and easy to thinly slice.

2 medium-size yellow squash (about 1 lb.), divided

2 medium zucchini (about 1 lb.), divided

2 medium carrots, divided

1 small onion, chopped

1 garlic clove, minced

3/4 cup vegetable broth, divided

5 Tbsp. olive oil, divided

1 tsp. table salt, divided

1/2 cup chopped fresh basil, divided

1 (4-oz.) package prosciutto, torn into strips

2 (8.8-oz.) packages pappardelle pasta

1 Tbsp. butter

3 green onions, chopped

1/2 (8-oz.) container mascarpone cheese

3/4 cup (3 oz.) freshly grated Parmesan cheese

TOP ⑤ PIZZAS & PASTAS

Summer Pasta

MAKES: 4 to 6 servings
HANDS-ON TIME: 30 min.
TOTAL TIME: 1 hour

❶ Cut 1 squash, 1 zucchini, and 1 carrot into 1/4-inch-thick slices. Place in a Dutch oven; add onion, garlic, 1/2 cup vegetable broth, 3 Tbsp. oil, and 1/2 tsp. salt. Cover and cook over medium-low heat, stirring occasionally, 20 to 30 minutes or until vegetables are very tender. Stir in 1/4 cup basil; cool 10 minutes.

❷ Meanwhile, sauté prosciutto in a lightly greased large nonstick skillet over medium heat 6 to 8 minutes or until browned and crisp; remove from skillet. Wipe skillet clean. Process cooked squash mixture and remaining 1/4 cup broth in a blender or food processor until smooth. Wipe Dutch oven clean.

❸ Cook pasta in Dutch oven according to package directions; drain, reserving 1 cup hot pasta water. Return pasta to Dutch oven. Cut remaining squash, zucchini, and carrot lengthwise into very thin, ribbon-like strips using a mandoline or Y-shaped vegetable peeler. Stack ribbons, and cut in half lengthwise. Melt butter with 1 Tbsp. oil in skillet over medium heat; add vegetable ribbons, green onions, and remaining 1/2 tsp. salt, and sauté 5 minutes or just until tender. Transfer to a plate; cover.

❹ Cook squash mixture, mascarpone cheese, and 1/4 cup Parmesan cheese 3 to 4 minutes or just until sauce is hot and cheese is melted. Pour sauce over pasta; toss to coat, adding desired amount of reserved hot pasta water to thin sauce, if necessary. Top with vegetable ribbons, prosciutto, and remaining 1/2 cup Parmesan cheese and 1/4 cup basil. Drizzle with remaining 1 Tbsp. olive oil.

test kitchen note

If you can't find pappardelle pasta, we suggest substituting fresh spaghetti or angel hair.

Grilled Pizza with Steak, Pear, and Arugula

MAKES: 4 servings
HANDS-ON TIME: 40 min.
TOTAL TIME: 50 min.

Vegetable cooking spray
1/2 lb. flank steak
1 Tbsp. olive oil
1 1/2 tsp. white balsamic vinegar
1 (12-inch) prebaked pizza crust
1 red Bartlett pear, peeled and sliced
1 1/2 cups fresh arugula, divided
1/4 cup crumbled Gorgonzola cheese
Freshly cracked pepper

❶ Coat cold cooking grate of grill with cooking spray, and place on grill. Preheat grill to 350° (medium heat).

❷ Season flank steak with salt and pepper to taste.

❸ Grill steak, covered with grill lid, at 350° (medium heat) 8 to 10 minutes on each side or to desired degree of doneness. Cover and let stand 10 minutes.

❹ Meanwhile, whisk together oil and vinegar in a small bowl.

❺ Cut steak diagonally across grain into thin strips. Cut strips into bite-size pieces (about 1 cup).

❻ Place pizza crust directly on hot cooking grate. Brush top of crust with oil mixture; layer with pear slices, 1 cup arugula, cheese, and beef strips.

❼ Grill, covered with grill lid, 4 minutes. Rotate pizza one-quarter turn; grill, covered with grill lid, 5 to 6 more minutes or until thoroughly heated. Remove pizza from grill, and sprinkle with remaining 1/2 cup arugula and freshly cracked pepper.

NOTE: We tested with 1/2 (16-oz.) package Mama Mary's Thin & Crispy Pizza Crusts.

community chat

Oooh, this is scrumptious! You can use goat cheese instead of the gorgonzola cheese, and the flavor is still wonderful. This is a fancy pizza—great for guests or a special family meal.

Chicken Parmesan Pizza

MAKES: 4 servings
HANDS-ON TIME: 15 min.
TOTAL TIME: 30 min.

1 (10-oz.) package frozen garlic bread loaf
1/2 cup canned pizza sauce
6 deli fried chicken strips

1 cup (4 oz.) shredded Italian three-cheese blend
2 Tbsp. chopped fresh basil

❶ Preheat oven to 400°. Arrange garlic bread, buttered sides up, on a baking sheet.

❷ Bake at 400° for 8 to 9 minutes or until bread is lightly browned. Spread pizza sauce over garlic bread.

❸ Cut chicken strips into 1/2-inch pieces, and arrange over pizza sauce. Sprinkle with cheese and basil.

❹ Bake at 400° for 8 to 10 minutes or until crust is golden and cheese is melted. Serve immediately.

make it a meal

Toss together romaine lettuce, freshly cracked pepper, and grated Parmesan cheese; toss with your favorite bottled Caesar dressing. Sprinkle with croutons for an easy side.

1 cup (1½-inch) diagonally cut asparagus (about ½ lb.)

1 (10-oz.) thin Italian cheese-flavored pizza crust

Vegetable cooking spray

2 Tbsp. commercial pesto

6 plum tomatoes, cut into ¼-inch-thick slices (about ¾ lb.)

1 cup (4 oz.) pre-shredded part-skim mozzarella cheese

¼ cup thinly sliced fresh basil

1 Preheat oven to 450°.

2 Steam asparagus, covered, 2 minutes or until crisp-tender. Rinse under cold running water; drain well, and pat dry with paper towels.

3 Place pizza crust on an ungreased pizza pan or baking sheet. Lightly coat pizza crust with cooking spray. Spread pesto evenly over crust. Arrange tomatoes and asparagus over pesto. Sprinkle with cheese. Bake at 450° for 15 minutes or until crust is golden and cheese is melted. Remove from oven, and sprinkle with basil.

4 Cut into 8 slices, and serve immediately.

Pizza with Tomatoes, Asparagus, and Basil

MAKES: 4 servings

HANDS-ON TIME: 17 min.

TOTAL TIME: 25 min.

shortcut secret

To quickly slice fresh basil, stack several leaves and roll them into a cylinder. Cut the cylinders crosswise with a sharp knife.

If you love a loaded pizza, try this recipe. Why it's better for you: The whole-wheat crust topped with roasted sweet potatoes and other colorful veggies ups the good-for-you factor!

Roasted Vegetable Pizza

MAKES: 4 servings

HANDS-ON TIME: 25 min.

TOTAL TIME: 1 hour, 40 min.

- 1 medium eggplant, peeled and cubed
- 1/4 tsp. table salt
- 2 medium zucchini, sliced
- 1 large sweet potato, peeled and cut into 1/2-inch cubes
- 1 onion, peeled and cut into eighths
- 1 red bell pepper, cut into 1-inch pieces
- 1/4 cup olive oil
- 1 Tbsp. chopped fresh rosemary
- 1/4 tsp. black pepper
- 1/2 (16-oz.) package whole-wheat prebaked pizza crusts
- 1 tsp. olive oil
- 1/3 cup shaved Asiago cheese

1 Sprinkle eggplant with salt, and let stand 30 minutes. Pat dry.

2 Preheat oven to 400°. Toss together eggplant, zucchini, and next 6 ingredients, and arrange in a single layer in 2 aluminum foil-lined 15- x 10-inch jelly-roll pans.

3 Bake at 400° for 45 minutes or until vegetables are tender and golden brown. Add salt to taste.

4 Place crust on a baking sheet. Brush crust with 1 tsp. oil. Top with 2 cups roasted vegetables; reserve remaining vegetables for another use. Sprinkle with cheese. Bake at 400° for 15 minutes or until crust is golden and cheese is melted.

test kitchen note

You can use more or less cheese, depending on what you have available.

Portobello Pizza

MAKES: 6 servings
HANDS-ON TIME: 22 min.
TOTAL TIME: 45 min.

2 large portobello mushroom caps, sliced*
1/2 large onion, sliced
1/2 tsp. table salt
1/2 tsp. black pepper
Vegetable cooking spray
1 Tbsp. balsamic vinegar
2 Tbsp. yellow cornmeal
1 (13.8-oz.) refrigerated pizza crust dough
2 Tbsp. commercial pesto
2 Tbsp. plain nonfat yogurt
1/4 cup chopped fresh basil
6 fresh mozzarella cheese slices (6 oz.)**
5 plum tomatoes, chopped
2 Tbsp. shredded Parmesan cheese

❶ Preheat oven to 425°. Sauté first 4 ingredients in a large skillet coated with cooking spray over medium-high heat 5 minutes or until onion is tender. Add vinegar; cook 2 minutes or until liquid is evaporated. Set aside.

❷ Sprinkle cornmeal over baking pan; spread out pizza dough. Bake on bottom oven rack at 425° for 5 minutes.

❸ Stir together pesto and yogurt. Spread over pizza crust, leaving a 1-inch border. Sprinkle with mushroom mixture and fresh basil. Top with mozzarella cheese and tomatoes. Sprinkle with Parmesan cheese.

❹ Bake at 425° on bottom oven rack for 18 minutes or until crust is golden and cheese is melted.

* 1 (8-oz.) package sliced button mushrooms may be substituted.
** 1 1/2 cups (6 oz.) shredded part-skim mozzarella cheese may be substituted.

test kitchen note

Baking the crust on the bottom rack will keep it from becoming soggy.

While it may sound like a fancy dish, Beef Lombardi is simply a mixture of ground beef and chopped tomatoes that's spooned over a mixture of creamy noodles, topped with cheese, and baked.

Beef Lombardi

MAKES: 6 servings

HANDS-ON TIME: 25 min.

TOTAL TIME: 50 min.

1 (8-oz.) package medium egg noodles

1 lb. lean ground beef

1¹/₂ tsp. salt, divided

¹/₂ tsp. dried Italian seasoning

1 (6-oz.) can tomato paste

1 (14¹/₂-oz.) can diced fire-roasted tomatoes

1 (3-oz.) package cream cheese, softened

¹/₂ cup sour cream

4 green onions, chopped

¹/₂ cup (2 oz.) shredded Italian six-cheese blend

1 Preheat oven to 350°. Prepare egg noodles according to package directions.

2 Meanwhile, sprinkle ground beef with 1¹/₄ tsp. salt and Italian seasoning. Cook beef in a large skillet over medium heat, stirring often, 5 to 6 minutes or until meat crumbles and is no longer pink.

3 Stir in tomato paste, and cook 2 minutes; stir in tomatoes, ¹/₂ cup water, and remaining ¹/₄ tsp. salt; reduce heat to medium-low, and simmer 8 minutes.

4 Microwave cream cheese in a microwave-safe bowl at HIGH 20 seconds. Stir in sour cream and green onions. Stir cream cheese mixture into hot cooked noodles.

5 Place noodle mixture in bottom of a lightly greased 11- x 7-inch baking dish. Top with beef mixture; sprinkle with cheese.

6 Bake at 350° for 25 minutes or until cheese is bubbly.

NOTE: To lighten, substitute low-fat or fat-free sour cream and 2% reduced-fat cheese.

shortcut secret

This is a great make-ahead dish because you can assemble the casserole and freeze it for up to one month.

Easy Lasagna

MAKES: 6 to 8 servings
HANDS-ON TIME: 30 min.
TOTAL TIME: 1 hour, 30 min.

1 lb. mild Italian sausage
1 (15-oz.) container part-skim ricotta cheese
¼ cup refrigerated pesto
1 large egg, lightly beaten
2 (26-oz.) jars pasta sauce
9 no-boil lasagna noodles
4 cups (16 oz.) shredded Italian three-cheese blend or mozzarella cheese

1 Preheat oven to 350°. Remove and discard casings from sausage. Cook sausage in a large skillet over medium heat, stirring until meat crumbles and is no longer pink; drain.

2 Stir together ricotta cheese, pesto, and egg.

3 Spread half of 1 jar pasta sauce evenly in a lightly greased 13- x 9-inch baking dish. Layer with 3 lasagna noodles (noodles should not touch each other or sides of dish), half of ricotta mixture, half of sausage, 1 cup three-cheese blend, and remaining half of 1 jar pasta sauce. Repeat layers using 3 lasagna noodles, remaining ricotta mixture, remaining sausage, and 1 cup three-cheese blend. Top with remaining 3 noodles and second jar of pasta sauce, covering noodles completely. Sprinkle evenly with remaining 2 cups three-cheese blend.

4 Bake, covered, at 350° for 40 minutes. Uncover and bake 15 more minutes or until cheese is melted and edges are lightly browned and bubbly. Let stand 15 minutes.

NOTE: We tested with Classico Tomato & Basil spaghetti sauce and Barilla Lasagne Oven-Ready noodles.

community chat

Scrape the layer of solidified oil from the top of the container of pesto, and discard. Then measure the pesto.

Crusty cheese bubbling over gratin dishes and hiding a thick meat sauce will please anyone at your dinner table.

Saucy Manicotti

MAKES: 7 servings

HANDS-ON TIME: 40 min.

TOTAL TIME: 1 hour, 30 min.

- 1 (8-oz.) package manicotti shells
- 1 (16-oz.) package Italian sausage, casings removed
- 1 large onion, chopped
- 9 garlic cloves, pressed
- 1 (26-oz.) jar seven-herb tomato pasta sauce
- 6 cups (24 oz.) shredded mozzarella cheese, divided
- 1 (15-oz.) container ricotta cheese
- 1 (8-oz.) container chive-and-onion cream cheese
- $^3/_4$ cup freshly grated Parmesan cheese
- $^3/_4$ tsp. freshly ground black pepper

❶ Cook manicotti shells according to package directions.

❷ Cook sausage, onion, and half of pressed garlic in a large Dutch oven over medium-high heat 6 minutes, stirring until sausage crumbles and is no longer pink. Stir in pasta sauce; bring to a boil. Remove from heat.

❸ Preheat oven to 350°. Combine 4 cups mozzarella cheese, next 4 ingredients, and remaining pressed garlic in a large bowl, stirring until blended. Cut a slit down length of each cooked manicotti shell.

❹ Spoon $^1/_4$ cup sauce into each of 7 lightly greased 8-oz. shallow baking dishes. Spoon cheese mixture into manicotti shells, gently pressing cut sides together. Arrange stuffed shells over sauce in dishes, seam sides down. Spoon remaining sauce (about $^3/_4$ cup per dish) over stuffed shells. Sprinkle with remaining 2 cups mozzarella cheese.

❺ Bake, uncovered, at 350° for 50 minutes.

community chat

This tasty dish can be made ahead. It's great for company.

Three-Cheese Baked Pasta

MAKES: 8 to 10 servings

HANDS-ON TIME: 10 min.

TOTAL TIME: 50 min.

1 (16-oz.) package ziti pasta

2 (10-oz.) containers Alfredo sauce

1 (8-oz.) container sour cream

1 (15-oz.) container ricotta cheese

2 large eggs, lightly beaten

¼ cup grated Parmesan cheese

¼ cup chopped fresh parsley

1½ cups (6 oz.) mozzarella cheese

1 Preheat oven to 350°. Cook ziti according to package directions; drain and return to pot.

2 Stir together Alfredo sauce and sour cream; toss with ziti until evenly coated. Spoon half of ziti mixture into a lightly greased 13- x 9-inch baking dish.

3 Stir together ricotta cheese and next 3 ingredients; spread evenly over pasta mixture. Spoon remaining pasta mixture evenly over ricotta cheese layer; sprinkle with mozzarella cheese.

4 Bake at 350° for 30 minutes or until bubbly.

shortcut secret

Prepare up to 1 day ahead; cover and refrigerate. Let stand at room temperature 30 minutes, and bake as directed. Ziti pasta is shaped in long, thin tubes; penne or rigatoni pasta may be substituted.

- ¹/₄ lb. thick bacon slices, diced (about 4 slices)
- 2 medium leeks, cut into ¹/₂-inch rounds (about 1 cup)
- ¹/₃ (16-oz.) package uncooked cavatappi pasta
- 1¹/₂ Tbsp. unsalted butter
- 1¹/₂ Tbsp. all-purpose flour
- 1 cup milk, warmed
- ¹/₂ tsp. dry mustard
- ¹/₄ tsp. table salt
- ¹/₄ tsp. ground black pepper
- Pinch of ground red pepper
- 1 cup (4 oz.) freshly grated 2-year-old aged Cheddar cheese, divided
- 1 egg yolk
- ¹/₂ cup freshly grated Gruyère cheese
- 2 Tbsp. heavy cream
- ¹/₄ cup toasted soft, fresh breadcrumbs

Southern Mac and Cheese

MAKES: 4 to 6 servings
HANDS-ON TIME: 45 min.
TOTAL TIME: 1 hour, 35 min.

1 Preheat oven to 375°. Cook bacon in a skillet over medium heat, stirring occasionally, 6 to 8 minutes or until crisp; remove bacon, and drain on paper towels. Discard drippings.

2 Cook leeks in 4 qt. boiling water in a large Dutch oven 5 minutes. Remove leeks with a slotted spoon, reserving boiling water in Dutch oven. Plunge leeks into ice water to stop the cooking process; drain.

3 Add pasta to boiling water, and cook 10 minutes or until al dente. Drain. Melt butter in a large skillet over medium heat. Reduce heat to medium-low, and whisk in flour until smooth; cook, whisking constantly, 2 minutes or until golden brown. Slowly whisk in milk, and cook, whisking constantly, 3 minutes or until thickened. Whisk in dry mustard, next 3 ingredients, and ¹/₂ cup Cheddar cheese, stirring until cheese is melted. Remove from heat. Add salt to taste.

4 Gently stir together pasta, cheese sauce, half each of cooked bacon and leeks, and egg yolk. Stir in Gruyère cheese and remaining ¹/₂ cup Cheddar cheese. Spoon pasta mixture into a buttered 8-inch cast-iron skillet, and sprinkle with remaining bacon and leeks. Drizzle with cream; sprinkle with breadcrumbs.

5 Bake at 375° for 35 minutes or until golden and bubbly. Let stand 15 minutes before serving.

shortcut secret

Place your bacon in the freezer for about 20 minutes before cutting it. It makes it just hard enough to easily slice.

Springtime Pasta with Bacon

MAKES: 6 to 8 servings
HANDS-ON TIME: 20 min.
TOTAL TIME: 30 min.

make it a meal

Enjoy this colorful dish warm or chilled; leftovers are perfect for a brown bag lunch the next day. Add grilled shrimp kabobs and a crisp Sauvignon Blanc for a relaxing meal with friends.

1 (16-oz.) package orecchiette pasta*
1 cup frozen sweet peas
1½ cups fresh snow peas
8 radishes, cut into wedges
2 large carrots, grated
2 green onions, thinly sliced
⅓ cup coarsely chopped fresh parsley
¼ cup lemon juice
¼ cup olive oil
6 thick bacon slices, cooked and crumbled
4 oz. crumbled goat cheese (optional)

❶ Cook pasta according to package directions, adding sweet peas and snow peas during last minute of cook time. Drain.

❷ Toss pasta mixture with radishes and next 5 ingredients; add salt and pepper to taste. Sprinkle with bacon and, if desired, crumbled goat cheese.

* 1 (16-oz.) package farfalle (bow-tie) pasta may be substituted.

1 (19-oz.) package frozen cheese tortellini

2 cups chopped cooked chicken

¼ cup sliced green olives

¼ cup sliced black olives

¼ cup diced red bell pepper

2 Tbsp. chopped sweet onion

2 Tbsp. chopped fresh parsley

2 Tbsp. mayonnaise

1 Tbsp. red wine vinegar

1 tsp. herbes de Provence*

¼ cup canola oil

Garnish: fresh parsley sprigs

Summer Tortellini Salad

MAKES: 4 servings

HANDS-ON TIME: 20 min.

TOTAL TIME: 45 min.

❶ Cook tortellini according to package directions; drain. Plunge into ice water to stop the cooking process; drain and place in a large bowl. Stir in chicken and next 5 ingredients.

❷ Whisk together mayonnaise, vinegar, and herbes de Provence. Add oil in a slow, steady stream, whisking constantly until smooth. Pour over tortellini mixture, tossing to coat. Stir in salt to taste. Cover and chill at least 25 minutes. Garnish, if desired.

* 1 tsp. dried Italian seasoning may be substituted.

community chat

This is perfect for a ladies salad supper. In a pinch, you can use fresh or frozen grilled chicken which will add even more flavor to the salad.

Pasta-Chicken-Broccoli Bake

MAKES: 6 to 8 servings
HANDS-ON TIME: 30 min.
TOTAL TIME: 1 hour, 15 min.

$^1/_2$ cup butter
$^1/_2$ cup chopped sweet onion
$^1/_2$ cup chopped red bell pepper
2 garlic cloves, minced
$^1/_4$ cup all-purpose flour
3 cups chicken broth
$1^1/_2$ cups half-and-half
$^1/_2$ cup dry white wine
1 cup (4 oz.) freshly shredded Parmesan cheese
$^1/_4$ tsp. table salt
$^1/_4$ tsp. ground red pepper
1 (20-oz.) package refrigerated cheese-and-spinach tortellini
4 cups chopped fresh broccoli
4 cups chopped cooked chicken
$^1/_2$ cup (2 oz.) grated Parmesan cheese
15 round buttery crackers, crushed
$^1/_2$ cup chopped pecans
3 Tbsp. butter, melted

❶ Preheat oven to 350°. Melt $^1/_2$ cup butter in a Dutch oven over medium-high heat; add onion and next 2 ingredients, and sauté 5 to 6 minutes or until tender.

❷ Add flour, stirring until smooth. Cook, stirring constantly, 1 minute. Whisk in broth, half-and-half, and white wine. Reduce heat to medium, and cook, stirring constantly, 6 to 8 minutes or until thickened and bubbly.

❸ Remove from heat; add 1 cup cheese and next 2 ingredients, stirring until cheese melts. Stir in tortellini and next 2 ingredients. Spoon into a lightly greased 13- x 9-inch baking dish.

❹ Stir together $^1/_2$ cup grated cheese and next 3 ingredients. Sprinkle over casserole. Bake at 350° for 40 to 45 minutes or until golden and bubbly.

NOTE: We tested with Buitoni Mixed Cheese Tortellini.

community chat

Stir the mixture several times to keep the tortellini cooking in the sauce.

Turkey Tetrazzini

MAKES: 2 servings
HANDS-ON TIME: 30 min.
TOTAL TIME: 30 min.

make it a meal

Serve this make-ahead casserole with green geans and rolls. Purchase bakery brownies for dessert.

1½ cups diced deli turkey breast (about ½ lb.)*
½ cup chopped onion
Vegetable cooking spray
¼ cup milk
1 (10¾-oz.) can cream of mushroom soup
¾ cup (3 oz.) shredded sharp Cheddar cheese
4 oz. spaghetti, cooked
2 Tbsp. chopped fresh parsley
Dash of black pepper
1 (2-oz.) jar diced pimiento, drained

❶ Sauté turkey and onion in a large nonstick skillet coated with cooking spray over medium-high heat 3 minutes or until onion is tender.

❷ Stir in milk, soup, and cheese; reduce heat to low, and cook, stirring constantly, 4 minutes or until cheese melts and mixture is smooth. Stir in spaghetti and remaining ingredients; cook 2 to 3 minutes or until thoroughly heated.

* Diced ham may be substituted.

Fast-and-Fresh Sausage Ragu

MAKES: 6 to 8 servings
HANDS-ON TIME: 40 min.
TOTAL TIME: 40 min.

- 1 (16-oz.) package rigatoni pasta
- 1 (1-lb.) package ground pork sausage with sage
- 1 medium onion, diced
- 1 medium zucchini, diced
- 2 medium carrots, diced
- 3 garlic cloves, pressed
- 1/4 tsp. dried crushed red pepper
- 1 (6-oz.) can tomato paste
- 1 cup dry red wine
- 1 (28-oz.) can diced tomatoes with basil, garlic, and oregano
- Freshly grated Parmesan cheese, basil

1 Cook pasta according to package directions; drain, reserving 1/2 cup hot pasta water.

2 Meanwhile, cook sausage in a large, 2-inch-deep skillet over medium-high heat, stirring often, 5 minutes or until sausage crumbles and is no longer pink. Add onion, zucchini, and carrots; cook, stirring often, 8 to 10 minutes or until tender. Add garlic and red pepper, and cook, stirring often, 1 to 2 minutes or until garlic is tender. Add tomato paste, and cook, stirring constantly, 1 to 2 minutes. Add wine and reserved pasta water; cook 2 minutes, stirring to loosen bits from bottom of skillet.

3 Add tomatoes, and bring to a boil. Reduce heat to medium, and simmer, stirring occasionally, 10 minutes. Add salt and pepper to taste. Spoon sausage mixture over pasta; sprinkle with cheese.

test kitchen note

Use your favorite breakfast or Italian sausage. For a finer texture, break up the sausage as it cooks using a potato masher.

Decadent Desserts

Ending a meal with a little something sweet can be a luxury during a busy week.

Making an apple pie has never been so easy. Simply toss apples, cinnamon, and brown sugar, and spoon over a refrigerated piecrust in a cast-iron skillet. Top with the other crust and bake.

TOP **5** DESSERT RECIPES

Easy Skillet Apple Pie

MAKES: 8 to 10 servings

HANDS-ON TIME: 20 min.

TOTAL TIME: 1 hour, 50 min.

- 2 lb. Granny Smith apples
- 2 lb. Braeburn apples
- 1 tsp. ground cinnamon
- 3/4 cup granulated sugar
- 1/2 cup butter
- 1 cup firmly packed light brown sugar
- 1 (14.1-oz.) package refrigerated piecrusts
- 1 egg white
- 2 Tbsp. granulated sugar

❶ Preheat oven to 350°. Peel apples, and cut into 1/2-inch-thick wedges. Toss apples with cinnamon and 3/4 cup granulated sugar.

❷ Melt butter in a 10-inch cast-iron skillet over medium heat; add brown sugar, and cook, stirring constantly, 1 to 2 minutes or until sugar dissolves. Remove from heat, and place 1 piecrust in skillet over brown sugar mixture. Spoon apple mixture over piecrust, and top with remaining piecrust. Whisk egg white until foamy. Brush top of piecrust with egg white; sprinkle with 2 Tbsp. granulated sugar. Cut 4 or 5 slits in top for steam to escape.

❸ Bake at 350° for 1 hour to 1 hour and 10 minutes or until golden brown and bubbly, shielding with aluminum foil during last 10 minutes to prevent excessive browning, if necessary. Cool on a wire rack 30 minutes before serving.

community chat

This was amazing and easy. It is delicious and again...EASY! Never buy a frozen pie again!

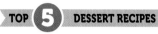

Nutter Butter® Banana Pudding Trifle

MAKES: 8 to 10 servings
HANDS-ON TIME: 55 min.
TOTAL TIME: 3 hours, 25 min.

3 cups milk
3 large eggs
$^3/_4$ cup sugar
$^1/_3$ cup all-purpose flour
2 Tbsp. butter
2 tsp. vanilla extract
5 medium-size ripe bananas

1 (1-lb.) package peanut butter sandwich cookies
2 cups sweetened whipped cream
Garnishes: peanut butter sandwich cookies, banana slices

❶ Whisk together first 4 ingredients in a large saucepan over medium-low heat. Cook, whisking constantly, 15 to 20 minutes or until thickened. Remove from heat; stir in butter and vanilla until butter melts.

❷ Fill a large bowl with ice. Place saucepan in ice, and let stand, stirring occasionally, 30 minutes or until mixture is thoroughly chilled.

❸ Meanwhile, cut bananas into $^1/_4$-inch slices. Break cookies into thirds.

❹ Spoon half of pudding mixture into a 3-qt. bowl or pitcher, or divide between 2 ($1^1/_2$- to 2-qt.) widemouthed pitchers. Top with bananas and cookies. Spoon remaining pudding mixture over bananas and cookies. Top with sweetened whipped cream. Cover and chill 2 to 24 hours.

NOTE: We tested with Nabisco Nutter Butter® sandwich cookies.

community chat

Yummy! This is one to definitely make again and again.

TOP **5** DESSERT RECIPES

Sour Cream Pound Cake

MAKES: 10 to 12 servings
HANDS-ON TIME: 20 min.
TOTAL TIME: 1 hour, 50 min.

test kitchen note

The addition of
sour cream makes
this pound cake
particularly
rich and tender.

1¹⁄₂ cups butter, softened
3 cups sugar
6 large eggs
3 cups all-purpose flour
¹⁄₂ tsp. table salt
¹⁄₄ tsp. baking soda
1 (8-oz.) container sour cream
1 tsp. lemon extract
¹⁄₄ tsp. almond extract

1 Preheat oven to 325°. Beat butter at medium speed with an electric mixer until creamy. Gradually add sugar, beating at medium speed until light and fluffy. Add eggs, 1 at a time, beating just until the yolk disappears.

2 Sift together flour, salt, and baking soda. Add to butter mixture alternately with sour cream, beginning and ending with flour mixture. Beat batter at low speed just until blended after each addition. Stir in extracts. Pour into a greased and floured 12-cup tube pan.

3 Bake at 325° for 1 hour and 20 minutes to 1 hour and 30 minutes or until a long wooden pick inserted in center of cake comes out clean. Cool in pan on a wire rack 10 minutes. Remove cake from pan, and cool completely on wire rack.

1 (18.9-oz.) package triple chunk brownie mix

1 bag assorted miniature peanut butter cup candies and chocolate-coated caramels

Preheat oven to 350°. Prepare brownie mix according to package directions. Spray miniature muffin pans with cooking spray, or line pans with paper liners, and spray liners with cooking spray. Spoon brownie batter into each cup, filling almost full. Bake at 350° for 19 to 20 minutes. Cool in pans 3 to 4 minutes, and then gently press a miniature candy into each baked brownie until the top of candy is level with top of brownie. Cool 10 minutes in pans. Gently twist each brownie to remove from pan. Cool on a wire rack.

Brownie Buttons

MAKES: 24 servings

HANDS-ON TIME: 15 min.

TOTAL TIME: 47 min.

shortcut secret

These brownies can be frozen ahead and brought out for a special dinner. Let brownies cool completely. Place in a zip-top plastic freezer bag; label and freeze up to 3 months. Thaw at room temperature.

1 cup butter, softened	2 cups all-purpose flour
$^3/_4$ cup powdered sugar	$^1/_4$ tsp. baking powder
2 tsp. vanilla extract	Dash of table salt
$^1/_2$ tsp. almond extract	Wax paper

Slice-and-Bake Shortbread Cookies

MAKES: 4 dozen

HANDS-ON TIME: 15 min.

TOTAL TIME: 5 hours, 15 min.

① Beat butter at medium speed with an electric mixer until creamy. Gradually add powdered sugar, beating until smooth. Stir in vanilla and almond extracts until blended.

② Stir together flour, baking powder, and salt. Gradually add flour mixture to butter mixture, beating at low speed until blended.

③ Shape shortbread dough into 2 (7-inch) logs. Wrap each log in wax paper, and chill 4 hours.

④ Preheat oven to 350°.

⑤ Cut each log into 24 slices. Place shortbread slices 1 inch apart on lightly greased or parchment paper-lined baking sheets.

⑥ Bake shortbread slices at 350° for 10 to 12 minutes or until edges of slices are golden.

⑦ Remove shortbread from baking sheets, and place on wire racks; cool completely (about 20 minutes). Store in airtight containers.

shortcut secret

Keep this dough frozen and pull it out to bake for a quick weeknight dessert.

Cranberry-Orange Shortbread Cookies:
Stir in $^1/_2$ cup chopped dried cranberries and 1 Tbsp. orange zest with extracts in Step 1.

Pecan Shortbread Cookies:
Omit almond extract. Stir in 1 cup finely chopped toasted pecans with vanilla in Step 1.

Strawberry Semifreddo Shortcake

MAKES: 16 servings
HANDS-ON TIME: 30 min.
TOTAL TIME: 5 hours, 45 min.

2 (3-oz.) packages soft ladyfingers
2 pt. strawberry ice cream, softened
1 pt. strawberry sorbet, softened
1 pt. fresh strawberries, hulled
2 Tbsp. powdered sugar
1/2 (7-oz.) jar marshmallow crème
1 cup heavy cream

❶ Arrange ladyfingers around sides and on bottom of a 9-inch springform pan. (Reserve any remaining ladyfingers for another use.) Spread strawberry ice cream over ladyfingers, and freeze 30 minutes.

❷ Spread softened strawberry sorbet over ice cream. Freeze 30 minutes.

❸ Process strawberries and powdered sugar in a food processor 1 minute or until pureed. Reserve 1/4 cup mixture. Whisk remaining strawberry mixture into marshmallow crème until well blended.

❹ Beat cream at high speed with an electric mixer until stiff peaks form. Fold into marshmallow mixture. Pour over sorbet in pan. Drizzle reserved strawberry mixture over top, and gently swirl with a paring knife. Freeze 4 hours or until firm. Let cake stand at room temperature 15 minutes before serving.

NOTE: We tested with Blue Bell Strawberry Ice Cream and Häagen-Dazs Strawberry Sorbet.

test kitchen note

Marshmallow crème stirred into this short-cake eliminates the traditional use for raw eggs. Ladyfingers make a pretty and tasty crust for this divine dessert. Look for soft ladyfingers in the bakery section of the grocery store.

A crisp, over-the-rim graham cracker crust spiked with ground cinnamon and red pepper adds a spicy cowboy kick to this showstopping pie.

Mexican Chocolate Ice-Cream Pie

MAKES: 8 servings
HANDS-ON TIME: 30 min.
TOTAL TIME: 10 hours, 50 min.

- 3 cups cinnamon graham cracker crumbs (about 22 whole crackers), divided
- $1/2$ cup butter, melted
- $1/4$ tsp. ground red pepper
- 1 (4-oz.) semisweet chocolate baking bar, finely chopped
- 1 (3.5-oz.) package roasted glazed pecan pieces
- 1 pt. chocolate ice cream, softened
- 1 pt. coffee ice cream, softened
- 1 cup whipping cream
- $1/4$ cup coffee liqueur

❶ Preheat oven to 350°. Stir together $2^{1}/_{2}$ cups cinnamon graham cracker crumbs and next 2 ingredients; firmly press mixture on bottom and up sides of a lightly greased 9-inch pie plate. Bake 10 to 12 minutes or until lightly browned. Cool completely on a wire rack (about 30 minutes).

❷ Stir together semisweet chocolate, pecan pieces, and remaining $1/2$ cup cinnamon graham cracker crumbs. Reserve $1/2$ cup chocolate-pecan mixture to top pie.

❸ Spread chocolate ice cream in bottom of prepared crust; top with remaining chocolate-pecan mixture. Freeze 30 minutes. Spread coffee ice cream over chocolate mixture. Cover and freeze 8 hours.

❹ Beat whipping cream and coffee liqueur at medium speed with an electric mixer until stiff peaks form. Spread whipped cream mixture over pie; sprinkle with reserved $1/2$ cup chocolate-pecan mixture. Cover and freeze 1 hour or until whipped cream is firm. Let stand 10 to 15 minutes before serving.

make it a meal

This pie makes a great ending to a Tex-Mex meal. Serve a favorite like enchiladas, fajitas, or tacos with Mexican rice and end the night with this pie for dessert.

Mocha-Pecan Mud Pie

MAKES: 9 servings

HANDS-ON TIME: 15 min.

TOTAL TIME: 8 hours, 35 min.

$^1/_2$ cup chopped pecans
Vegetable cooking spray
1 tsp. sugar
1 pt. coffee ice cream, softened
1 pt. chocolate ice cream, softened
1 cup coarsely chopped cream-filled chocolate sandwich cookies, divided (about 10 cookies)
1 (6-oz.) ready-made chocolate crumb piecrust
2 Tbsp. chocolate syrup

❶ Preheat oven to 350°. Place pecans in a single layer on a baking sheet coated with cooking spray; sprinkle with sugar. Bake for 8 to 10 minutes or until lightly toasted, stirring halfway through. Cool.

❷ Stir together ice creams, $^3/_4$ cup cookie chunks, and $^1/_3$ cup pecans; spoon into piecrust. Freeze 10 minutes. Press remaining cookie chunks and pecans on top. Cover with plastic wrap, and freeze 8 hours.

❸ Drizzle individual slices with chocolate syrup.

NOTE: We tested with Keebler Chocolate Ready Crust, Häagen-Dazs Light Coffee Ice Cream, Häagen-Dazs Light Dutch Chocolate Ice Cream, and Oreo Cookies.

shortcut secret

Use a food processor to coarsely chop the cream-filled chocolate sandwich cookies.

Parchment paper

Devil's food cake batter

1/2 gal. mint chocolate chip ice cream, softened

10 chocolate wafers, coarsely crushed

Chocolate ganache

Garnishes: sweetened whipped cream, thin crème de menthe chocolate mints

Mint Chocolate Chip Ice-Cream Cake

MAKES: 10 to 12 servings

HANDS-ON TIME: 30 min.

TOTAL TIME: 10 hours, 30 min., including batter and ganache

❶ Preheat oven to 350°. Grease and flour 3 (8-inch) round cake pans. Line with parchment paper. Prepare devil's food cake batter, and spoon into pans.

❷ Bake at 350° for 12 to 14 minutes or until a wooden pick inserted in center comes out clean. Cool in pans on a wire rack 10 minutes. Remove from pans to wire racks, peel off parchment paper, and cool completely (about 1 hour).

❸ Place 1 cake layer in a 9-inch springform pan. Top with one-third of ice cream (about $2^1/_3$ cups); sprinkle with half of crushed wafers. Repeat layers once. Top with remaining cake layer and ice cream. Freeze 8 to 12 hours.

❹ Remove cake from springform pan and place on a cake stand or plate. Prepare chocolate ganache, and spread over top of ice-cream cake. Let stand 15 minutes before serving.

Chocolate Ganache:

Microwave 1 (4-oz.) semisweet chocolate baking bar, chopped, and 4 Tbsp. whipping cream in a microwave-safe bowl at HIGH 1 minute or until melted, stirring at 30-second intervals. Stir in up to 4 Tbsp. additional cream for desired consistency. Use immediately. **HANDS-ON TIME:** 5 min.; **TOTAL TIME:** 5 min.

community chat

Let everyone drizzle their own ganache over this amazing dessert.

Mississippi Mud Cake

MAKES: 15 servings

HANDS-ON TIME: 15 min.

TOTAL TIME: 40 min.

1 cup butter
4 oz. semisweet chocolate, chopped
2 cups sugar
1 1/2 cups all-purpose flour
1/2 cup unsweetened cocoa
4 large eggs
1 tsp. vanilla extract
3/4 tsp. salt
1 (10.5-oz.) bag miniature marshmallows
Chocolate frosting
1 cup toasted chopped pecans

❶ Preheat oven to 350°.

❷ Microwave butter and semisweet chocolate in a large microwave-safe glass bowl at HIGH 1 minute or until melted and smooth, stirring every 30 seconds.

❸ Whisk sugar and next 5 ingredients into chocolate mixture. Pour batter into a greased 15- x 10- x 1-inch jelly-roll pan.

❹ Bake at 350° for 20 minutes. Remove from oven, and sprinkle evenly with miniature marshmallows; bake 8 to 10 more minutes or until golden brown. Drizzle warm cake with chocolate frosting, and sprinkle evenly with toasted pecans.

Chocolate Frosting:

1/2 cup butter
1/3 cup unsweetened cocoa
1/3 cup milk
1 (16-oz.) package powdered sugar
1 tsp. vanilla extract

Stir together first 3 ingredients in a medium saucepan over medium heat until butter is melted. Cook, stirring constantly, 2 minutes or until slightly thickened; remove from heat. Beat in powdered sugar and vanilla at medium-high speed with an electric mixer until smooth.

MAKES: 2 cups; HANDS-ON TIME: 10 min.; TOTAL TIME: 10 min.

community chat

Great recipe! It makes a lot so you may have leftovers for days!

2 Tbsp. granulated sugar
2 cups Quick & Easy
  Lemon Curd, divided
2 Tbsp. all-purpose flour
1/8 tsp. table salt

4 large egg whites, at
  room temperature
1/8 tsp. cream of tartar
2 Tbsp. powdered sugar

Lemon Soufflés

MAKES: 5 (4-oz.) servings

HANDS-ON TIME: 15 min.

TOTAL TIME: 4 hours, 50 min., including curd

❶ Preheat oven to 400°. Lightly coat 5 lightly greased 4-oz. ramekins with granulated sugar, shaking out excess. Place on a jelly-roll pan. Whisk together 1 cup lemon curd, flour, and salt in a large bowl.

❷ Beat egg whites with tartar at medium speed with an electric mixer 1 to 2 minutes or until soft peaks form. Gently fold one-fourth of egg white mixture into curd mixture using a rubber spatula; fold in remaining egg whites just until blended. Pour into ramekins, filling to top. Run tip of thumb around edges of ramekins, wiping clean.

❸ Bake at 400° for 10 minutes; reduce heat to 350°, and bake 4 minutes or until soufflés rise and are set. (Center should be slightly loose when shaken.) Dust with powdered sugar. Serve immediately with remaining lemon curd.

Quick & Easy Lemon Curd:

Grate zest from 6 lemons to equal 2 Tbsp. Cut lemons in half; squeeze juice into a measuring cup to equal 1 cup. Beat ½ cup butter and 2 cups sugar at medium speed with an electric mixer until blended. Add 4 eggs, 1 at a time, beating just until blended after each addition. Gradually add lemon juice to butter mixture, beating at low speed just until blended after each addition; stir in zest. (Mixture will look curdled.) Transfer to a 3-qt. microwave-safe bowl. Microwave at HIGH 5 minutes, stirring at 1-minute intervals. Microwave, stirring at 30-second intervals, 1 to 2 more minutes or until mixture thickens, coats the back of a spoon, and starts to mound slightly when stirred. **MAKES:** 2 cups; **HANDS-ON TIME:** 15 min.; **TOTAL TIME:** 15 min.

shortcut secret

Prep the lemon curd up to 2 weeks ahead and you can serve these in just 30 minutes.

Chocolate Coffee Cheesecake Truffles

MAKES: 15 tartlets

HANDS-ON TIME: 30 min.

TOTAL TIME: 2 hours, 38 min.

2 Tbsp. slivered almonds
1 (2.1-oz.) package frozen mini-phyllo pastry shells, thawed
2 Tbsp. heavy cream, divided
½ tsp. instant espresso powder
1 (3-oz.) package cream cheese, softened
3 Tbsp. powdered sugar
2 Tbsp. light brown sugar
1 oz. bittersweet chocolate

❶ Preheat oven to 350°. Place almonds in a single layer in a shallow pan. Bake at 350°, stirring occasionally, 5 to 7 minutes or until lightly toasted and fragrant.

❷ Place thawed pastry shells on a baking sheet, and bake at 350° for 3 to 5 minutes or until crisp.

❸ Stir together 1 Tbsp. cream and espresso powder in a small microwave-safe ramekin or cup. Microwave at HIGH 10 seconds; stir until espresso is dissolved.

❹ Beat cream cheese and sugars at medium-high speed with an electric mixer until smooth. Gradually add espresso mixture, and beat 30 seconds or until creamy and light. Spoon 1 rounded teaspoonful into each phyllo shell.

❺ Microwave chocolate and remaining 1 Tbsp. cream in a small microwave-safe ramekin or cup at HIGH 20 seconds, stirring after 10 seconds and at end until smooth. Spoon ¼ tsp. chocolate mixture over each tart.

❻ Top immediately with almonds. Cover and chill 2 hours or up to 24 hours.

shortcut secret

You can quickly soften the cream cheese by completely removing it from the wrapper. Place it on a microwave-safe plate and heat on HIGH for 10 seconds or until softened.

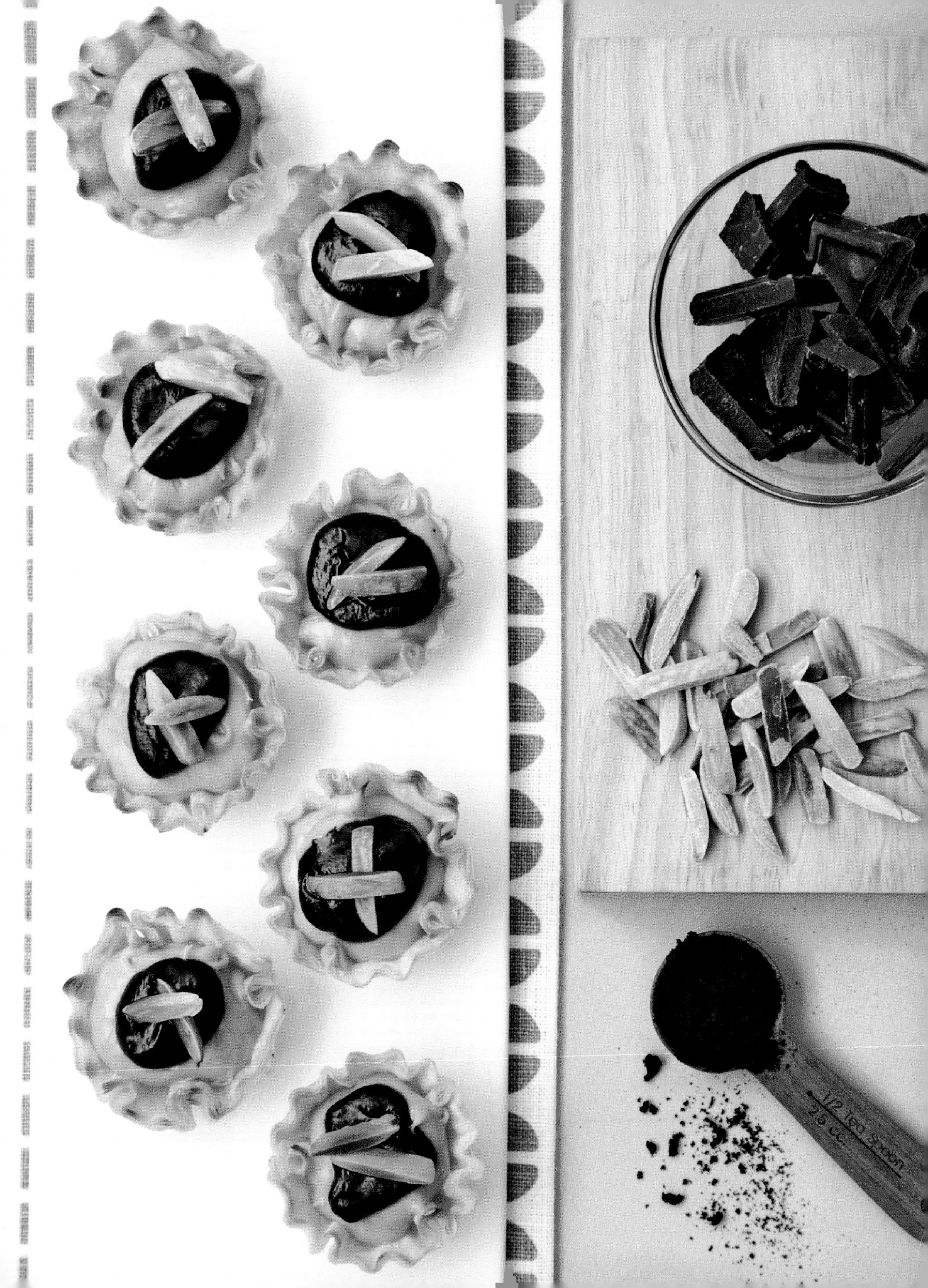
1/2 Tea Spoon
2.5 cc.

Best-Ever Brownies

MAKES: 2¹/₂ dozen

HANDS-ON TIME: 20 min.

TOTAL TIME: 3 hours, 40 min.

1 (8-oz.) package unsweetened chocolate baking squares, chopped
1¹/₂ cups butter, cut up
4 cups sugar
2 cups all-purpose flour
6 large eggs
1 Tbsp. plus ¹/₈ tsp. salt
1 Tbsp. vanilla extract
Edible gold leaf (optional)

1 Preheat oven to 350°. Line a 13- x 9-inch pan with aluminum foil, allowing 2 inches to extend over sides; lightly grease foil.

2 Bring 1 inch of water to a simmer in bottom of a double boiler. Place chocolate and butter in top of double boiler. Cook, stirring occasionally, 5 to 6 minutes or until melted. Cool 10 minutes; transfer to a large bowl. Stir in sugar until blended. Stir in flour and next 3 ingredients just until blended. Pour batter into pan.

3 Bake at 350° for 32 to 35 minutes or until set. Cool in pan 30 minutes. Freeze 2 hours; cut into squares or triangles. Press tops with gold leaf, if desired.

test kitchen note

These are super fudgy. For a more cake-like brownie, bake 5 to 7 minutes longer.

Watermelon Granita

MAKES: about 7 cups
HANDS-ON TIME: 20 min.
TOTAL TIME: 8 hours, 35 min.

8 cups seeded and cubed watermelon

1 (6-oz.) can frozen orange juice concentrate, thawed

1½ cups lemon-lime soft drink

1 Process watermelon in a blender or food processor until smooth.

2 Stir together watermelon puree and remaining ingredients. Pour mixture into a 2-qt. glass bowl. Cover and freeze 8 hours, stirring occasionally.

3 Remove from freezer 15 minutes before serving. Stir with a fork, and spoon into glasses. Serve immediately.

NOTE: We tested with 7Up soft drink.

make it a meal

Enjoy a family cookout with hamburgers, chips, and coleslaw. Serve this make-ahead dessert as a sweet ending.

Metric Equivalents

The information in the following charts is provided to help cooks outside the United States successfully use the recipes in this book. All equivalents are approximate.

EQUIVALENTS FOR DIFFERENT TYPES OF INGREDIENTS

Standard Cup	Fine Powder	Grain	Granular	Liquid Solids	Liquid
	(ex. flour)	(ex. rice)	(ex. sugar)	(ex. butter)	(ex. milk)
1	140 g	150 g	190 g	200 g	240 ml
¾	105 g	113 g	143 g	150 g	180 ml
⅔	93 g	100 g	125 g	133 g	160 ml
½	70 g	75 g	95 g	100 g	120 ml
⅓	47 g	50 g	63 g	67 g	80 ml
¼	35 g	38 g	48 g	50 g	60 ml
⅛	18 g	19 g	24 g	25 g	30 ml

LIQUID INGREDIENTS BY VOLUME

¼ tsp				=	1 ml
½ tsp				=	2 ml
1 tsp				=	5 ml
3 tsp	= 1 Tbsp =		½ fl oz	=	15 ml
	2 Tbsp =	⅛ cup =	1 fl oz	=	30 ml
	4 Tbsp =	¼ cup =	2 fl oz	=	60 ml
	5⅓ Tbsp =	⅓ cup =	3 fl oz	=	80 ml
	8 Tbsp =	½ cup =	4 fl oz	=	120 ml
	10⅔ Tbsp =	⅔ cup =	5 fl oz	=	160 ml
	12 Tbsp =	¾ cup =	6 fl oz	=	180 ml
	16 Tbsp =	1 cup =	8 fl oz	=	240 ml
	1 pt =	2 cups =	16 fl oz	=	480 ml
	1 qt =	4 cups =	32 fl oz	=	960 ml
			33 fl oz	=	1000 ml = 1 l

LENGTH

(To convert inches to centimeters, multiply the number of inches by 2.5.)

1 in			= 2.5 cm	
6 in =	½ ft		= 15 cm	
12 in =	1 ft		= 30 cm	
36 in =	3 ft =	1 yd	= 90 cm	
40 in			= 100 cm	= 1 m

COOKING/OVEN TEMPERATURES

	Fahrenheit	Celsius	Gas Mark
Freeze Water	32° F	0° C	
Room Temperature	68° F	20° C	
Boil Water	212° F	100° C	
Bake	325° F	160° C	3
	350° F	180° C	4
	375° F	190° C	5
	400° F	200° C	6
	425° F	220° C	7
	450° F	230° C	8
Broil			Grill

DRY INGREDIENTS BY WEIGHT

(To convert ounces to grams, multiply the number of ounces by 30.)

1 oz =	1/16 lb =	30 g
4 oz =	¼ lb =	120 g
8 oz =	½ lb =	240 g
12 oz =	¾ lb =	360 g
16 oz =	1 lb =	480 g

Index

Pasta and Noodles

America's Best Recipes Simple Weeknight Meals

Editor: Susan Hernandez Ray
Project Editor: Emily Chappell Connolly
Assistant Designer:
  Allison Sperando Potter
Recipe Developers and Testers:
  Wendy Ball, R.D.; Victoria E. Cox;
  Tamara Goldis; Stefanie Maloney;
  Callie Nash; Karen Rankin;
  Leah Van Deren
Recipe Editor: Alyson Moreland Haynes
Food Stylists: Margaret Monroe Dickey,
  Catherine Crowell Steele
Photography Director: Jim Bathie
Senior Photographer: Hélène Dujardin
Senior Photo Stylist: Kay E. Clarke
Photo Stylist: Mindi Shapiro Levine
Assistant Photo Stylist:
  Mary Louise Menendez
Production Managers:
  Theresa Beste-Farley, Sue Chodakiewicz

CONTRIBUTORS
Project Editor: Jena Hippensteel
Designer: Claire Cormany
Compositor: Frances Gunnells
Recipe Developers and Testers:
  Erica Hopper, Tonya Johnson,
  Kyra Moncrief, Kathleen Royal Phillips
Copy Editors: Susan Kemp, Barry Smith
Proofreader: Rebecca Benton
Interns: Morgan Bolling, Megan Branagh,
  Sara Lyon, Staley McIlwain, Jeffrey Preis,
  Maria Sanders, Julia Sayers

OXMOOR HOUSE
Editorial Director: Leah McLaughlin
Creative Director: Felicity Keane
Brand Manager: Katie McHugh
Senior Editor: Rebecca Brennan
Managing Editor: Elizabeth Tyler Austin

©2013 by Time Home Entertainment Inc.
135 West 50th Street, New York, NY 10020

ISBN-13: 978-0-8487-4243-0
ISBN-10: 0-8487-4243-5

Library of Congress Control Number:
  2013945629
Printed in the United States of America
First Printing 2013

TIME HOME ENTERTAINMENT INC.
Publisher: Jim Childs
VP, Brand & Digital Strategy:
  Steven Sandonato
Executive Director, Marketing Services:
  Carol Pittard
**Executive Director, Retail & Special
  Sales:** Tom Mifsud
**Director, Bookazine Development &
  Marketing:** Laura Adam
Executive Publishing Director: Joy Butts
Associate Publishing Director:
  Megan Pearlman
Finance Director: Glenn Buonocore
Associate General Counsel: Helen Wan

To order additional publications, call
1-800-765-6400 or **1-800-491-0551.**

For more books to enrich your life, visit
oxmoorhouse.com

To search, savor, and share thousands
of recipes, visit **myrecipes.com**

Cover: Fast-and-Fresh Sausage Ragu,
  page 253